THE COMPLETE GUIDE TO TRAINING A NEW PUPPY

STEP BY STEP GUIDE FOR BEGINNERS INCLUDING HOUSE, POTTY AND CRATE TRAINING, LEASH, RECALL AND SEPARATION ANXIETY.

HELEN SUTHERLAND

TWENTY DOGS PUBLISHING

© Copyright Twenty Dogs Publishing 2021 - All rights reserved.

The content contained within this book may not be reproduced, duplicated or transmitted without direct written permission from the author or the publisher.

Under no circumstances will any blame or legal responsibility be held against the publisher, or author, for any damages, reparation, or monetary loss due to the information contained within this book. Either directly or indirectly. You are responsible for your own choices, actions, and results.

Legal Notice:

This book is copyright protected. This book is only for personal use. You cannot amend, distribute, sell, use, quote or paraphrase any part, or the content within this book, without the consent of the author or publisher.

Disclaimer Notice:

Please note the information contained within this document is for educational and entertainment purposes only. All effort has been executed to present accurate, up to date, and reliable, complete information. No warranties of any kind are declared or implied. Readers acknowledge that the author is not engaging in the rendering of legal, financial, medical or professional advice. The content within this book has been derived from various sources. Please consult a licensed professional before attempting any techniques outlined in this book.

By reading this document, the reader agrees that under no circumstances is the author responsible for any losses, direct or indirect, which are incurred as a result of the use of the information contained within this document, including, but not limited to, errors, omissions, or inaccuracies.

Subtitle

The essential positive recall and leash training guide. Includes all the training cues including come, heel, sit, stay and the emergency stop

Author: Helen E. Sutherland

CONTENTS

INTRODUCTION	1
1. WELCOME HOME	5
Before you bring your puppy home	5
What's in a name?	7
He's arrived!	8
Socialization	9
Vaccinations over the first year	10
2. HOUSE AND POTTY TRAINING	13
How long can a puppy wait for the toilet	14
Puppy Pads	15
How to manage their potty training	16
Where?	17
The signs to watch out for	18
Leaving the house and overnight	20
How to clean up the mess	20
Create a Schedule	21
Your schedule	21
Sleep	22
Bedtime	23
3. CRATE TRAINING	24
Introducing your pup to the crate	25
Size and Types of Crate	29
4. FOOD AND FEEDING	32
What to feed them	32
How much to feed	34
What not to feed - dangerous foods for your dog	35
What to do if your pet is poisoned	37
5. CHEWING AND MOUTHING	39
Mouthing	39
Chewing	42

6. RECALL TRAINING PREPARATION ... 45
   Basic Training ... 48
   Getting to know his name ... 49
   Look at Me ... 49
   Teach him to Sit ... 50
   Teach him to Lie Down ... 51
   Teach him to stay or wait ... 52
   Leash training ... 52

7. THE FOUNDATIONAL CUES ... 54
   Decide on your cue ... 55
   Sit Stay and Release ... 56

8. RECALL TRAINING ... 58
   Get him used to coming to you ... 59
   Training sit-stay ... 60
   Sit stay come ... 60
   Going Outside - enclosed area ... 61
   Using the long-line ... 63
   Using a Clicker ... 66
   Recall Summary and where the Clicker fits in ... 67
   Proofing ... 69
   Emergency stop ... 70
   What not to do ... 71

9. GOING TO THE PARK ... 74
   Other dogs and their communication signals ... 76
   How dogs greet each other ... 77
   How to interact with humans ... 79
   Games ... 80

10. LEASH AND HEEL TRAINING ... 82
    How to hold the leash ... 82
    Walking to heel ... 83
    Establish the heel position ... 83
    Start walking ... 85
    Meeting other dogs while on the leash ... 86

11. SEPARATION ANXIETY ... 88
    Not all dogs are the same ... 90
    Causes and Signs Of Separation Anxiety ... 91

What to watch out for	94
Why Punishment Won't Work	95
Preparation and Socialization	96
How to leave and return	99
Leaving when using a crate	102
Some other useful tips	102
The 10 Steps to help Separation Anxiety	103
12. WHAT BREED IS RIGHT FOR YOU?	105
Sporting	105
Hounds	106
Herding Dogs	107
Working Dogs	108
Terriers	108
Toy Dogs	109
Non-Sporting	109
Do you have an allergy?	110
Do you have children?	110
Do you have time for lots of exercise?	110
How strong are you?	111
Do you have neighbors nearby?	111
13. CONCLUSION	112
14. NEED MORE HELP?	115
15. LEAVE REVIEW	117
Resources	119

INTRODUCTION

I grew up with dogs and was often involved in their training. I watched every dog training programme I could and read almost every book on the subject that I could.

Training was very different then. In those days it was believed that punishment and fear was the best way to train a dog. We were told that you had to be the leader and that your puppy was trying to dominate you if if did things you didn't want it to do. I can still remember holding a rolled-up newspaper to our pet dog Paddy and I shudder at that image today.

In most cases he was getting into trouble because he had ran away - the fear was ours and we were terrified he would run across the busy road near our house and get hit by a car.

When I think about it now, recall training was not something that featured much in our training when he was a puppy. We did heel and come and he was good on the lead (it was choke chains in these days).

Our next family dog was a springer spaniel, and by that time training was moving on a little. But it was still fear-based but to a lesser degree. It was still about dominance over our dogs. I would watch the various training programmes on TV and wonder how the dog must feel and what it was supposed to understand. But most of all I wondered what the puppy or dog would be thinking.

It took me a while to feel ok about getting my own dog and I realised I had to learn about training all over again. I worried about it - how would I house train, how would I get her to come back.

As a lay beside Millie the day she came home with me, I just cuddled her and thought about my responsibility to ensure she had a great life - that my home was a great choice for her and one she would be happy with.

Of course, as the first days went by the list of training needs grew and grew. How could I get her to stop chewing everything? How often and for how long should I walk her, how long could I leave her and how could I prevent her pulling on the leash. How could I tell if another dog was a threat or not?

I didn't want a highly trained dog - I just wanted one that knew what to do and that I felt was safe and able to enjoy herself when we went for a walk. As ever, I researched and read everything and tried many things until I found what worked best.

As time went by and the second puppy came along (the son of Millie) I wanted to know more about leash and recall.

Barney was the first male dog I had had since Paddy, and I was terrified he would run away like Paddy had done. This all eventually lead me to go through accredited dog training courses, including one specifically on leash and recall. To me, this is still the most under-rated aspect of puppy training - it can save his life.

One of the biggest changes over the years has been the recognition around the importance of early socialization - it is the easiest of things to do but can have such a big impact on your lives together. Separation and anxiety is also much better understood today.

But perhaps the biggest change has been the move to reinforcement or operant training. This is the realm of training that I believe works much better, and it is now supported by an abundance of animal behavioural research.

Not only is it great for your puppy, but he will learn faster and learn better. I don't go into all the behavioural aspects around, for example, the 4 quadrants but you will find these elements in the training. I also talk about using visual cues as well as vocal ones, and I would encourage you to try to introduce visual cues as much as you can.

In this book, I explain the essential training that dog trainers learn and that every puppy parent needs to know.

Training should involve all of the family, adults and kids alike. Everyone in your puppy's home is a parent.

The training will start as soon as your puppy is home, and it will show your puppy how to live in your home and be happy and content.

It will help him want to do everything that you need him to do and enable your puppy to spend as much time with you as possible, everywhere and anywhere, and ensure he has the perfect life with you - even if sometimes, you are not at home.

THIS BOOK INCLUDES TRAINING ON:

- How to potty train and house-train your puppy
- Crate Training and the best size of crate
- Eating and examples of poisonous everyday food
- How to get your puppy to pay attention
- Indoor and enclosed recall training
- Sit, stay, and come
- Walking to heel
- Leash and recall Training
- Proofing

- Emergency stop
- Going to the park
- Causes of Separation Anxiety
- How to prevent Separation Anxiety

Sometimes it feels like there is too much to learn, but if you follow the training and go through each stage step-by-step, it will be fun and easy and it won't take as long as you think!

1

WELCOME HOME

The first thing to know about puppy training, and also dog training, is that you will make mistakes. And the second thing to know is that your puppy will do things that you don't expect.

Each dog is unique, and each one will have its own way of doing things, which means that even although you have done everything right, it just won't work for your puppy in the way you thought it would.

But I promise you, these unique traits will be things that you will love the most about your pup. You will look out for these things and adore them because this is what makes him your special dog.

Before you bring your puppy home

Find out what type of food your puppy has been eating up until this point. You will want to introduce him to the food you want to use slowly, and you will do this by mixing some of his existing food into the new food you have for him.

The reason you do this is that a sudden change in diet will upset his tummy, and not only make him feel uncomfortable but can lead to unexpected accidents that the puppy just won't be in control over and make it more difficult in the first few days to start potty training successfully.

You will also want to know when (and how often) your puppy is used to being fed.

To change his food, start with a small amount of his new food mixed into what he is used to, then slowly increase the amount until all of his food is the food you have chosen.

This is a rule that you will follow throughout his life. Dogs - and their stomachs - don't like a sudden change to their diet, so always introduce a new dog food slowly, no matter how old your dog is.

The next thing you want to try and do, is have something that smells like his previous home. If the current owner or breeder doesn't have something you can take home with you, then ask if you can leave some clothing there for a week or so before you bring him home (a sock or an old towel).

This will give your puppy some comfort over the first few days, and be a familiar smell for him. Ideally, put this in his crate or the basket you want him to use when he gets home.

Finally, if you have a garden, you will need to puppy-proof it. I can promise you, if there are any gaps in a fence or hedge, your puppy will find it, and he will disappear in a second to go exploring. Use chicken-wire or something similar.

Anything will do as long as it can securely block access. I kept the chicken wire there for over a year and removed it bit-by-bit, checking to see if the young dog (he's called Barney) noticed the area beyond the garden that could be just within reach. (I still watch him, even now, and he is already 5 years old!). Millie, the older dog, was never too bothered by what might be next door, but Barney was always curious as a puppy.

Remember, mixing in some games with the potty and crate training is a great way to get the kids, and everyone else, involved in the care of your new puppy. This means before your puppy arrives, think about who can do what and try and get the family or other household members involved as early as you can (this is also good for helping to prevent separation anxiety).

And don't forget to pick the name of your puppy! You will want to know this as soon as he gets home so you can start training him by using it.

What's in a name?

Your puppy might already have a name, but if you are reading this before you have picked your puppy's name, then there are a few ways to decide on his name that can make training easier.

For example, the best names end with a vowel sound. This is because dogs hear at a higher frequency range than we do, and so this grabs the attention better. Ideally his (or her) name should start with a hard letter sound like B or D rather that perhaps Shep, and it should contain two syllables.

But remember, you want to avoid any names that your puppy might confuse with one of your cue's or commands (like sit, stay, here or come).

Try and say the name a few times too because you need to make sure all the members of your family can say it -especially if they are toddlers - and that they are happy to use it in the park.

Don't worry if you take a day or two to find just the right name that seems to fit who your puppy is. If you have a dog from a shelter, and you really want to change his name, or don't know what his name used to be, then give him a few days to get used to it (but it might take him a bit longer).

To get him used to his name, say it, and reward him when

you say it even when there is no response. Then, as soon as there is a response, immediately reward with a tastier treat. Just walk around the house and say his name and reward his response. Getting your puppy used to their name can be fun for us all.

He's arrived!

When your pup comes home, you will ideally already have his crate or basket ready. You will have the same type of dog food that he was being fed, and you will have the item placed in his crate or basket that smells like his previous home.

Over the first few nights, he is likely to miss his old family. It is okay over these first nights to take his crate or basket into your room, but only do this for the first few nights.

He also won't be used to lots of noise and activity around him. Try and keep things as calm as possible, and make sure to create some 'time-outs' for him.

To introduce him to his crate, place it in the room with you and where you tend to spend most of your time. If you have a room you want your puppy to stay in, then, after a day or two move the crate into this room - but make sure you also spend time there with him.

Don't forget that puppies sleep a lot. They also need their sleep, so try and let them have their sleep time even though everyone will want to play with your new puppy and pick them up and cuddle them. This is okay, and it is actually great for the puppy to have lots of affection, and integrate into the entire life of his new family, so just be aware of it.

In terms of picking them up and cuddling them, try not to overdo their handling, especially if they have not been used to it. Constantly picking them up will be something their little bodies are not used to, and, just like us, if we get picked up too much, it can become uncomfortable and even sore.

This isn't anything to worry too much about, but it's handy to be aware of how often they are being handled. And, of course, being picked up by different people gets them used to other people from an early age.

The best way to pick up your puppy is to put your hands between his front legs and around his chest. Then pull him towards your chest and, at about the same time, and when he is safely secured, take one of your hands and use it to support his bottom so that you are supporting his weight.

Finally, don't forget to take a sniff of his breath! A puppy's breath has a unique smell, so grab your chance while you can! It disappears quickly, and I would not recommend doing this later, when the smell may not be quite so sweet!

As mentioned earlier, puppies sleep a lot. They will easily sleep for 7-8 hours at night, and they will generally sleep up to 14 hours a day. I will talk about a schedule later, and it will include sleep time for him.

Socialization

In its simplest form, socialization is how you and your puppy learn to communicate with each other and how your puppy learns about others that he lives with and meets.

Having as many happy encounters as possible during his early weeks helps him to relate appropriately to humans of all ages, other dogs and to the situations that he will face day-to-day throughout his life.

Your puppy's first few weeks are really important for his socialization training, but this isn't easy in the first week or two because your puppy has yet to be vaccinated.

However, you can still carry him, take him out in your car, and have others come to the house to meet him. Try and let him meet as many adults and children as you can, in the weeks before you can take him to classes. He should also meet other dogs at home if you know them, and you know that they are fully vaccinated.

This is also the best time to touch their ears, mouth, tails, and paws and to get him used to you doing this. This part of training is often missed, but it will really help later with grooming, or if you need to inspect him for any injury.

Sit with him quietly so that you are also teaching him how to relax with you, and touch his ears or mouth, run your hand over his paws and his tail, and give him a treat and reward him when he remains calm and relaxed.

If you can, and as soon as you are allowed, and after his vaccinations allow it, take your puppy to socialization classes where he can meet other young puppies and their parents.

They will play around for 20 or 30 minutes, but they learn how to communicate with other dogs that they don't know and how 'far they can go.'

They also learn about meeting other humans who are not the family.

This part of his early training helps him feel comfortable with other dogs, and meeting and interacting with other people, and it really will be invaluable.

Vaccinations over the first year

It's a good idea to talk to your vet about your puppy's vaccination requirements as soon as you can. Below is a summary of the recommended vaccinations from the American Kennel Club, and there are also optional vaccinations that you can give your puppy.

I have only highlighted the recommended vaccinations here.

- 6-8 weeks - Distemper, parvovirus

- 10-12 weeks - DHPP (for distemper, adenovirus (hepatitis), parainfluenza, parvovirus
- 16-18 weeks DHPP, rabies
- 12-16 months DHPP, rabies

Unvaccinated puppies less than 4 months old are most at risk of Parvovirus. Parvovirus is contagious and affects all dogs. There is no cure, and the puppy will need to be kept hydrated, and an effort made to control the secondary symptoms.

The Kennel Club recommends talking to your veterinarian about Heartworm treatment when your puppy is 12-16 weeks old. This is a preventative medication that is taken regularly.

These are the sort of issues where any recommendation must come from a qualified pet health professional who understands the laws, and problems in your area, and who will be aware of any breed-specific problems. Make sure that you ask your veterinarian for advice.

Your puppy can go outside for a walk in the park after his third set of vaccinations (around weeks 16-18). It is also at this point that he can exercise for up to 20 minutes at a time.

He can also now meet unfamiliar dogs. Before this, you can take him to your yard around 7 days after his first set of vaccinations, but avoiding other dogs. Your yard must be enclosed to ensure no other dogs have been there. His feet must also not touch the ground in public spaces.

If you live in an apartment, you might need to do this during potty training and to let your puppy relieve himself outside. Pick one spot, and carry him there and back, and you can let him sniff around that spot.

After his second vaccination, you can take him for a walk on paved surfaces, but not on grass or places where you can't see if other dogs have urinated or gone to the toilet, although I would also suggest that you carry him, rather than walk him, on any surface.

It is still important for them not to meet unfamiliar dogs. It is at this stage, when he is just under 18 weeks, that you can take him to his puppy socialization classes at the local pet store or your vet (where all the other puppies will be at the same vaccination stage).

2

HOUSE AND POTTY TRAINING

One of the main reasons people don't want to have a puppy is the thought of potty training, or specifically, the thought of a dog that is not house-trained.

House training or potty training your puppy will be one of the first things you do when your puppy comes home. It can be done, so don't worry, but there will be a few accidents along the way. And that's okay too.

It won't last for long, and the benefits of having your pup with you for the years that follow are well worth the odd mishap or two. In fact, you will forget that you had to house-train and even how you did it.

The speed at which your pup learns will vary and can also depend on where he came from or if any training has already started in his previous home.

I know this sounds obvious, especially if you have an adopted puppy, but even a young puppy's rate of being house trained will depend on what they were taught once they were weaned and walking confidently on their 4 legs.

When we had a litter of 7 spaniels, we started to train the puppies to go to the puppy pad we had on the floor as soon as they reached the stage of moving around and were occasionally getting to venture outside.

We used puppy pads, and we started by moving the pads closer to the door and eventually outside. This meant that when they went to their forever homes, they were easy to train and complete the house training.

They were also used to using a cage kept in the room with them and where they could wander in to play and sleep (and get used to its sound). It really can help a great deal.

How long can a puppy wait for the toilet

Don't forget that a puppy's bladder grows with them. So when they are younger, it is smaller, which means that they will need to empty it more often.

Generally speaking, a puppy's ability to hold its bladder increases by about an hour per month.

This will mean that at one month, they can hold on for about an hour. By 2 months old, they should be able to hold on for about 2 hours before they need to relieve themselves.

Try not to make them hold on for much more than this over the first few months, or there will be accidents, and try to make sure that your time away from them can tie into their need to go toilet.

As a general rule, puppies under 6 months will struggle to hold their bladder for more than 3 or 4 hours, and this should help you work out how long you can be away or when you might need to try and get someone to visit your puppy so that they can relieve themselves outside, rather than in their crate, or in the room they are in.

In terms of pooping, a puppy will poop after food. If you feed your puppy before you leave, make sure that you feed them around 45 minutes before you are due to leave.

This gives you time to take them for a poop. They will

normally need to poop between 5 and 30 minutes after a meal. Millie used to poop about 5 minutes after her meal, while Barney was about 20 minutes.

If you are playing with your puppy before you leave, take them out for a poop after the playtime, as this can also make them want to poop.

Puppy Pads

The best thing I have used for potty training is puppy pads and the very best thing I ever tried was a puppy pad that looked like grass. For some reason, it really works. I used it with the seven puppies before they left for their forever homes, and they all used it.

Whether you use a fabric pad or a fake grass one, these are the things you need to do.

I started by placing the puppy pad in the room as soon as my puppy, Millie, came home. Then, when she looked like she was about to potty, I would place her on the pad, and if she relieved herself, she got lots of praise.

After that, it didn't take much time before she would go to the pad, probably around 2 days.

I then started to move the puppy pad towards the door I wanted her to use to go out. Try not to move it too far from where you started the training; just move it slowly to the door.

Once at the door, I let her get used to that for a day or two then I moved the pad just outside the door.

In the final stages, if I saw her starting to pee or potty, without going outside, I would gently pick her up and place her on the pad, and then I would take her and the pad outside. If there was not enough time to do this, I would just place her on the pad.

You might want to consider placing the puppy pad at the door he will be using to access his outside area right away. Of course, this will depend on how far from the room the household congregates is from that door.

At every point, give your puppy lots of praise.

This process can take more time than it might need to. However, as long as you remember that he will want to relieve himself when he wakes up, after play, or after he eats, you have a head-start knowing when to expect activity.

It's important never to punish or get angry with your puppy if he toilets in the house. You sometimes see a recommendation to push their face into the mess. Don't do this. It will do the opposite of helping.

They won't understand and will be scared. Getting angry or pushing them may only mean that they don't want to potty in front of you and learn to avoid it.

How to manage their potty training

Puppy's (and later dogs) love praise and rewards.

Once your puppy begins the process of going outside to potty, don't forget that every time he relieves himself outdoors, you need to praise him and give him a treat.

Don't do this while he is in the action of potty-time—he will stop to seek the reward, get distracted, and won't finish what he started, which means that he won't be fully relieved when he goes back inside. Instead, wait until he has finished, and don't forget to do this every single time he goes outdoors to potty.

As you do this, use a phrase that he will start to recognize (try not to use 'Good boy' or 'Good girl' - it might cause confusion!). I used to say 'Be a good girl' and, on reflection, this wasn't a great idea.

Instead, use a short phrase such as 'potty' or 'poo poo' or whatever you feel comfortable saying and will remember—just make sure it is one that your pup can begin to recognize with the action he is being asked to complete. This is a key step because they need to know exactly what behavior the reward is for.

This is not only useful when your puppy is young. Millie, my older dog, had soft tissue damage to her knee on her hind leg. This meant that she struggled to walk and had difficulty 'sitting down' to toilet.

When I carried her to the garden to try and get her to 'do pee-pee,' this was much easier because I could say a phrase, and she knew exactly what I wanted her to do.

Although she tried her best to 'poo-poo,' she didn't manage this for over a day, but I was greatly relieved when she finally 'pee-peed.'

Because I could ask her what to do, she knew what to try to do. It's good to remember that much of what you teach now will be of great help throughout your puppy's life. It's also good to think about what phrase you will be stuck with for a long time!

Where?

Choose a place or a small area outside where you want him to relieve himself. As he relieves himself, say your word or a specific phrase.

Always take him to the same place every time you take him out to potty - in the morning, the last thing at night, after food, or after play during the day.

If you are using training pads overnight, take the soiled pad to the area where you want your puppy to toilet. The scent can help him.

When it is time to take him outside to toilette, avoid playing with him and getting him excited before he relieves himself. Remember, he is easily distracted and will forget what he is there to do.

If your puppy looks a bit confused or doesn't toilet right

away, just try to encourage him to sniff the ground beside the area you want him to use.

Stay outside with him until he toilettes. If nothing happens after 5 minutes, take him back inside but watch him closely.

After 10 minutes, take him out again and repeat the process until he has done what you need him to do.

The signs to watch out for

Try and supervise your puppy all of the time when you are trying to potty train him. I know this is very hard to do as they tend to have a mind and vision of their own.

By supervising and watching him, you will notice not only how he looks when he starts to feel uncomfortable because his bladder is full, but you will notice how he reacts when this happens.

For example, he might start circling or sniffing the floor, he might be restless, and he may try and go to a place where he has previously done his business.

If you see your puppy mid-toilet, pick him up and take him outside and try to get him to finish what he started there; if he does, then gently praise him.

Now, this is hard to describe, and I don't think I have ever seen it written down, but watch your puppy's bottom.

When they need to go poop, you will notice their rear end swelling outwards. This means a poop is imminent. To this day, I watch Millie and Barney's rear ends when we are out walking (usually it's the start of a walk), and I get the poop bags ready.

Millie always goes at the start of the walk or at the end. Barney is often too excited to play at the start, but mid-walk, he starts to seek out clumps of grass or trees. He prefers something to poop 'on.'

As you will learn or already know, puppies and dogs are all a bit different in how they prefer to poop and pee.

When Millie was a puppy, she was obviously getting restless and looking around for a place to pee-pee. In terms of poops, she is less discerning. She still behaves like this today. Barney will pee-pee anywhere, but he is very careful about where he poops.

When he was a puppy, Barney just looked a 'certain way' and eventually started moving towards the door, but he never actually 'asked' out.

He still does this—he never asks out vocally. He just stands beside the door without making any noises, whereas Millie whines.

When Barney was young, he was really difficult to read because he didn't do any obvious things like scratching at the door, sniffing, or circling.

When he was younger, the poops always came as a surprise to him. He would go for a pee-pee and suddenly discover a poop was coming. He was always surprised by this and, to this day, I get the impression that poops remain a surprise!

He now has a short sharp bark if he is really desperate and I haven't already noticed him patiently standing beside the door, but that's it. He will quietly wait silently for as long as he can and then give his bark.

Watch out for any of those signs, or watch out for something your dog does that might signal a change in behavior in how they are feeling. Watch their bottoms as sometimes, like Barney, they don't even know what's coming.

This is the part where they train us. We need to watch and learn what they are telling us. As soon as you notice any of these things, then take them outside. If they relieve themselves, then follow up with your praise and treats.

Some trainers would advise that the dog is tethered in the home on a long leash - around 6 feet. I don't think this needs to be the case. I am not even sure I think that it should ever be done or recommended. It simply can't be a good way to train your puppy or teach him about his home. I have never tethered any dog in the house.

I would, though, recommend keeping them to just one or two rooms as you go through the house-training process—be vigilant; watch, learn, and stay with them if you can, but don't tether them.

Leaving the house and overnight

Your puppy won't be able to hold his bladder all night long for several months. This means it is likely that he will need to go during the night.

Put some newspaper or puppy pads in his crate but try and place them in an area that he can avoid. In the morning, don't forget to take the soiled pad or newspaper to his garden area.

If you are going out for any length of time, then do the same thing but try, if you can, to be no more than 2-3 hours at the start.

It may take several months before your puppy is fully house trained, but the accidents will become less frequent. Try and be patient. It will pay off in time, and in just a few short years, you will have forgotten all about the trials and tribulations of potty training your puppy.

How to clean up the mess

It's important to clean the area and try to remove the scent.

Don't use ammonia-based products as this will just encourage them to go to the same place again. I have found that cold water can do the trick, too (and it is very good at removing any staining). You can use biological powder, and some people swear by a vinegar-water mix. I have tried this, but I am not convinced it works, although I know other dog owners where this has worked wonders.

Create a Schedule

One of the best and most effective ways to train your puppy is to get him used to a schedule.

The key aspects of your schedule will be feeding times, sleeping time (puppies like to sleep a lot), and of course, potty time.

Your schedule

When you first bring your puppy home, make sure that you take them out frequently. Take them out as soon as they wake up, after playing, and after they have eaten or had a drink.

A useful summary of what you need to do is detailed in these 5 steps:-

1. Feed them at the same time
2. Feed them with the same frequency, for example, every 2 hours depending on their age
3. Take them out them out as soon as they wake up
4. Take them out before they go to bed
5. Take them out after food and after play.

In terms of how a day might look, try not to forget his sleep time. Your puppy will get sleepy after eating.

Just make sure that you take him out to potty right after he has eaten but before he goes for his first morning nap.

I tend to let my dogs out as soon as they wake up. I then feed them breakfast and play with them for 20-30 minutes (depending on how much time I have), then I take them out again before they fall asleep. They have been doing this schedule since they were young pups, and they seem to like it. These days, as adults, they potty either when they wake up or after breakfast.

Sleep

As mentioned earlier, puppies sleep a lot. When he is young and up to 3 months old, he can sleep18 hours a day, sometimes up to 20!

He can fall asleep suddenly, and it can even appear as if he has fallen asleep mid-step. He will fall asleep with a chew in his mouth or just sit down in the middle of the floor and collapse. When he does, just pick him up and put him in his crate or basket (with the door open).

He should easily sleep for 7 hours at night, and some puppies can sleep for 7 hours without requiring a bathroom break.

Puppies need their sleep, so make sure you don't forget to let him get it. This will be harder than you think in the first few weeks. There will be many visitors and lots of people who will want to pick him up and cuddle him. This is okay but don't forget to give him his sleep time. He needs it.

Build this into your schedule so that it might look like this:

7 AM - WAKE up and go outside
    7:30 am - breakfast
    7:45 am - playtime
    8:00 am - outside for toilet
    8:15 am - sleep (with toy in the cage/depart for work?)
    10:15 am - outside for toilet
    10:30 - food
    10:40 - outside for toiler
    10:50 - playtime
    11:10 - outside for toilet
    11:15 am - sleep with Kong or Toy in the cage
    1:15pm - wake up/ outside for toilet
    1:20pm - food

1:25 - outside for toilet/playtime
1:30 - playtime
2:00 pm - outside for toilet
2:15 - sleep (cage with toy)

AND SO ON. You will find a schedule that works for you as you discover when your pup likes to go potty during the day. It might be after food or after playtime. But always take him out as soon as he awakens.

At the end of the day, it will be outside for the toilet, then to his cage or basket.

These timings will change as he gets a bit older and sleeps less—but he will always sleep a great deal, up to 14 hours a day.

Bedtime

You will find that your puppy will start to go to bed by himself. He will get used to your schedule and will fit into when you go to bed at night.

In the early days, if he does wake up during the night, don't make a fuss and do not be tempted to play with him. He will be more than happy to play, but he needs to learn that this is not the right time. Don't turn on all the lights either. Keep things like 'night time.' Take him outside to let him toilet and then return him to his bed.

Dogs should always have access to water. However, at night, and about one to two hours before he goes to bed, remove his water bowl (make sure he has had a recent drink first, he needs his water).

3

CRATE TRAINING

Many people worry that using a crate might be cruel. If used properly, a crate is a place that your puppy will feel safe and happy. This is the main objective of your crate training.

It brings a range of other benefits that will mean your life with your puppy can be as full and as engaging as possible - and allow him to be included in almost all of your activities, and even holidays.

The most important use of a crate is to provide a safe place for your puppy. Never use the crate as punishment or as a 'sin bin.'

Crate training is often one of the main ways to help speed up house training.

The reason using the crate works for potty training is that dogs don't like to mess where they sleep, and where they relax.

The puppy will not mess here, especially if you have crate trained him to view his crate as his safe place. What's more, if he is sleeping in his crate, he will do his very best to hold on until he can leave his crate.

This puts you in more control, because you will know

where your puppy is, and what he might want to do, when you open the door or when he leaves his crate.

This means as soon as your puppy leaves his crate (or you let him out), take him outside to relieve himself. He will soon get used to this routine, especially when he gets his praise and reward.

Crate training has lots of other benefits. Your dog will be able to travel with you more easily, in the car or on a plane. You can visit friends and family more easily because you can use the crate as their portable den.

You can go out knowing that you won't return to chewed furniture or a general mess (the chewing usually only occurs with puppies), and your dog can use the crate as his bed and sleep there overnight.

In summary, the crate gives your dog and puppy somewhere safe to rest and to sleep. It helps them feel comfortable when you leave the house; they can feel safe in a new house or room that you both are visiting, and it means that your dog can enjoy more of your life outside of the home if you need to travel.

It also helps them settle with a dog sitter if they need to go and stay away from home when you go on vacation.

Introducing your pup to the crate

After picking your crate, and before the puppy arrives, add a blanket or something soft for your puppy to lie on.

If you are using a second-hand crate, make sure you wash it thoroughly to remove any scent of the previous dog who may have been using it.

If you are using a wire crate, have something like a sheet or a blanket, that you can place on top of, and on the sides of, his crate. Don't cover up all four sides, and make sure the front of the crate (where the door is) is left uncovered. This can help to make it feel more like a den, especially at night.

A puppy will not be used to being alone, and it will make him anxious and scared, especially when he first arrives at his new home.

Initially, you can place the crate in a room that is used by the rest of the household. This will help the puppy get used to the crate without being separated from you, and your puppy's new family, and it will mean he doesn't feel alone and scared.

If you want to, you can put the crate into the room that you want him to use and then follow the steps below. Once you pick your room make sure that you also spend lots of time there with him.

When your puppy comes home, place his toys, and the item from his previous home, into the crate.

The first stage is to place some food around the crate. If he doesn't start moving towards the crate, or being curious about it all by himself, then entice him by calling him to the crate in a happy tone of voice, and by throwing tasty treats around and near the crate. Keep trying until he starts to come over to the crate and begins to feel comfortable around it.

The next stage is to slowly start moving the treats to the door, and then inside the crate. Give him lots of praise at all stages. Only start moving the food inside the crate once he has started getting used to the outside of the crate. As he starts to enter the crate, don't close the door.

Keep playing the game and move the treats or food deeper into the crate. Just let him enter and leave and explore if he wants to. You want to get him used to entering and leaving by himself.

It can take anything from 10 minutes to a few days, depending on his experience to date, to get him to go into his crate by himself. Keep the training sessions to between 3 and 5 minutes.

If your puppy is not responding to food and treats for any reason, then entice him with his favorite toy (some dog breeds prefer toys to treats).

The next phase is to increase the length of time he spends in his crate. You can do this by feeding him in his crate, or you can put a Kong toy filled with treats into the cage, for him to play with.

If he is reluctant to go into the crate, put his food bowl beside the crate door, and then slowly move it into the crate until he eats at the back of the crate.

Once he is happy entering and leaving and lingering for a few minutes in his crate, try to close the door. You can do this when he is eating, but one of the most effective ways is to give him his Kong stuffed with something he loves.

Wait until he starts to become engrossed in getting his food out of the Kong, then slowly close the door. If you close the door and he gets anxious or scared, immediately open the door.

If he does nothing, then wait for a few minutes before opening the door again.

Keep increasing the length of time before you open the door—you want to try and reach 10 minutes. If he shows any signs of distress, if he is panting, whining, cowering, or showing any signs of aggression, then you will know you have increased the time too quickly.

Once your puppy is happy to stay in the crate up to 10 minutes after eating or playing, then you will know that he is now likely to understand that his crate is a safe space.

The next phase of his crate training can now begin, and this is when you move out of sight, while he is in his crate with the door closed.

This is the stage when his toys and his Kong (filled with food, peanut butter, or soft cheese) will really help.

Put his toys in his crate, and close the door once he has

entered. Stay beside the crate for around 5 minutes before moving quietly from the room and out of sight.

Once you are out of sight, turn around and come back to the side of the crate and sit beside it for 5 minutes. Gradually start to stay out of sight longer. Do this throughout the day but at different times. You will need to repeat the process several times.

If you hear any barking or whining, do not come back mid bark or mid whine. Try and find a gap, and this is when you return. You are aiming to increase the time you are out of sight to around 30 minutes.

Once this has been achieved, you can start leaving the house altogether. But remember to provide toys for him to play with, so that he does not get bored. Before leaving, make sure he has had a small meal and has been exercised, and remember to leave calmly without any fuss.

In terms of sleeping at night, you can put the crate in your bedroom at night in the early days. You only want to do this for a few days—not any longer.

When your puppy first arrives home, he will have been used to sleeping with other puppies, so letting him sleep in his crate in your room will help him settle in.

Once you put the crate into the room where he will spend his time at night, make sure to turn out the lights when you (and he) go to bed. You can leave a low-level one on if you like, but make sure it isn't bright.

This will also mean that if you need to take them out during the night, they will recognize that this is sleep time. And don't forget that if you need to take them out during the night, don't turn on all the lights.

Size and Types of Crate

There are 3 main types of crate. A plastic crate (or box), a wire crate or cage, and one made of fabric—I think of this as a travel carry case that can be used both as a safe place and for travel.

Most of my experience is with a cage and a fabric crate, but I know many people who use a plastic crate. This choice is up to you.

What size?

Unlike the crate's material, the size of the crate you choose is important.

If the crate is too small, it will make your dog uncomfortable, and it is too big, it can make your dog insecure. You need to know the height, width, and length of the crate (or kennel).

The easiest thing to do is get an idea of how big your puppy will grow to be. If you are training an older dog (or a dog over 12 months old), measure from the top of his nose to the base of his tail. It's also a good idea to measure the height of your dog when he is sitting down.

To estimate the crate size, you will need to add around 2 to 4 inches to your measurement for height and 1 to 2 inches for the length. The width is less important as it will relate to the height.

The next thing you need to do is check your dog's weight or, in terms of your puppy, check the average weight of his breed when fully grown. Then make sure to check the weight limits on the crate you are buying (or you may be able to pick it up from another dog owner who is no longer using their crate).

Finally, to save you from buying different crates as your puppy grows, you can section off a part of the crate with a separator to make it smaller when he is smaller.

DOG BREED SIZING, HEIGHT AND WEIGHTS

Below are the general crate sizes by dog breed size. Check with your breeder or veterinarian on your dog's expected final height and weight (some dogs can be smaller or larger than the averages noted below). This is a useful guide from Copper's Crates that is a good starting point.

Extra Small Dog Breeds 18" – 22" Dog Crate

Toy breeds weighing up to 10 lbs and up to 12" in height

Examples only: Boston Terrier, Chihuahua, Jack Russell, Pug, Shih Tzu

Small Dog Breeds 24" Dog Crate

Dogs weighing between 11-25 lbs and 3"-17" in height.

Example only: King Charles Spaniel, Dachshund, French Bulldog

Medium Dog Breeds 30" Dog Crate

Dogs weighing between 26-40 lbs and between 18"-19" in height.

Examples only: American Pit Bull Terrier, Cocker Spaniel, Dachshund, Miniature Schnauzer, Wheaten Terrier

Intermediate Dog Breeds 36" Dog Crate

Dogs weighing between 41-70 lbs and from around 20"-22" in height.

Examples only: Alaskan Husky, Basset Hound, Beagle, Border Collie, Cocker Spaniel, English Setter, English Springer Spaniel, Siberian Husky, Standard Schnauzer, Whippet

. . .

LARGE DOG BREEDS 42" Dog Crate
Dogs weighing between 71-90 lbs and about 23" - 26" in height.
Examples only: Australian Shepherd, Boxer, Dalmatian, English Setter, German Shepherd, Golden Retriever, Irish Setter, Labrador Retriever, Rhodesian Ridgeback, Poodle (Standard)

EXTRA LARGE DOG BREEDS 48" Dog Crate
Dogs weighing between 91 - 110 lbs and ranging from around 26" - 28" in height
Examples only: Afghan Hound, Akita, Alaskan Malamute, Bernese Mountain Dog, Bloodhound, Doberman Pinscher, Giant Schnauzer, Greyhound

XXL GIANT DOG BREEDS 54" Dog Crate
Dogs Weighing over 110 lbs and ranging from somewhere between 29" - 40" in height
Examples only: Great Dane, Irish Wolfhound, Mastiff, Newfoundland, St. Bernard

4
FOOD AND FEEDING

As you might expect, feeding and pooping are closely related! You need to get your puppy into a regular schedule. The quicker you can do this and get him used to this schedule, the easier everything becomes. Creating a schedule really can make a big difference.

Feeding them to the same schedule also means that they will want to relieve themselves in reaction to that schedule. This, in itself, will make it easier for you to house-train.

What to feed them

Dogs are built to be meat-eaters, but they are descended from omnivores, so they can survive adequately without meat (if the protein balance is right).

The protein in meat is not the same as the protein found in plant-based foods, and this is one of the reasons to be careful of the food you give your puppy and your dog.

This doesn't mean that dogs can't live on a plant-based diet;

it just means it will need to be supplemented with the essential proteins he will require and Vitamin D.

Balancing nutrition is the most important aspect of your dogs' food. For example, we need our carbs for energy, but dogs don't need many carbs.

Dogs, and especially puppies, need fats and fatty acids. Most of these are contained in animal fats, but some seed and plant oils can provide a concentrated source of energy. You are looking for an Omega-3 family of essential fatty acids.

When looking for dog food, look at the type of calories rather than the overall total. For example, you don't want too much carbohydrate.

Today's average dog food can contain anywhere between 30% and 70% carbohydrates, but in the wild, dogs will intake only about 15%.

An adult dog's diet can contain up to 50% carbohydrate (by weight), up to 4.5% fibre, and a minimum of around 5.5% should come from fats, and 10% from protein.

You can read more about nutrition at nap.edu, and this is listed in the resources at the end of this book.

In general, though, if you want to check out how much meat is in your dog food, look at the ingredients list. The further down the meat appears, the lower the meat content.

The most common ingredients today are whole grain, fat, soya, and corn. So if you see chicken by-products, this doesn't mean it is chicken meat. It most likely isn't.

The top ingredients to look for (and look for a range of these in the same food) include deboned chicken or turkey, Atlantic mackerel and herring, chicken and turkey liver, chicken and turkey heart, and other items such as egg and other types of fish. All high in protein.

There has also been some debate about dry food versus wet food. The main difference being that wet food contains more water (around 75%) whereas dry food can contain only about 10% water.

Dry food tends to be more calorie-dense, and wet food has less grain and fewer carbs. Grain isn't necessarily a bad thing; it just depends on quantity.

Dry food lasts for longer and tends to be more cost-effective than wet food.

There are lots of choices on the market, and you will want to research this yourself. I feed Millie and Barney wheat-free dry fish-based kibble, but I try to change this from time to time. I have now found a brand that they love. It comes from a local farm producer.

Sometimes, I mix in some wet food. They really love this, and I quite like the mix of wet and dry food as a balance. It's also important to add some things in now-and-again to give your dog a little change.

How much to feed

Puppies can require up to double the energy intake of adult dogs. This is based on weight - it doesn't mean they eat twice as much as an adult dog, just that per pound of weight they do - and they weigh a lot less when they are puppies.

Small breeds of dogs can reach their adult weight in nine to twelve months. Medium, large and giant-breed puppies can eat too much at this stage, and this might lead to bone or joint problems later. This means it is best to control their feeding and not leave food in their bowl for them to nibble on between meals.

The frequency really does depend on how old they are. A puppy's tummy is small when he arrives home and will grow over time. The means you need to feed smaller amounts more regularly.

Puppies aged 8-16 weeks need to be fed 4 meals a day,

perhaps every 3 hours. Pups ages 3 to 6 months should be fed 3 times a day (every 4 hours) and then after that twice a day, in the morning and early evening.

Your aim is to spread their nutrition throughout the day, so space out the times to equal intervals across the day. Remember not to feed your puppy just before or after their walk (or playtime).

The amount that you feed your puppy will depend on their weight and age. The dog food you choose will also have a variety of different protein levels.

When you decide on your dog food, the packaging will tell you how much to feed your puppy, depending on their weight. If you are in any doubt, ask your veterinarian.

What not to feed - dangerous foods for your dog

ALCOHOL - under no circumstances give your dog alcohol. In the worst-case scenario, alcohol can cause death.

CAFFEINE AND CHOCOLATE—don't give your puppy anything with caffeine. Things that can include caffeine are obviously coffee, but chocolate can also contain caffeine. Chocolate, especially dark chocolate, should never be given to your dog. The toxic substances can cause vomiting, irregular heart function, and even death. If your dog has eaten a lot of chocolate, contact your veterinarian immediately.

COCONUT (including coconut oil) - in small quantities, might cause stomach upsets, but coconut water should not be given to your dog.

HOPS are used in the process of brewing beer. If you are a home-brew enthusiast, then you must keep hops out of the reach of your German Shepherd. Signs to look out for are increased breathing, a racing heart rate, and vomiting. In severe cases, death can occur.

ONION, CHIVES, AND GARLIC can irritate the bowel and are toxic to dogs.

NUTS (Pecans, Almonds, Walnuts, Macadamia) - these have the potential to not only cause vomiting but possible pancreatitis.

RAISINS AND GRAPES - avoid giving your dog raisins or grapes. The effect the toxins have is still not definitive, but it can cause Kidney failure. This also includes other dried variants like sultanas and currants and any foods containing grape, such as grape juice, raisin cereal, raisin bread, granola, trail mix, and raisin cookies or bars. Early signs are vomiting, diarrhea, and lethargy.

RAW POTATO (or green potato) is poisonous to dogs. It contains a toxic compound called solanine (which is also contained in GREEN TOMATO'S), and if your dog eats a large amount, it will affect his nervous system. Symptoms to look for are blurred vision, vomiting, diarrhea, low temperature, and slow heart rate.

TURKEY AND CHICKEN BONES. Generally speaking, be careful of any bones that you give your dog to chew. If they can easily break them apart, they can lodge in their throats or their intestines. Even lamb joint bones can be dangerous for dogs who can chew through them, and they can be quite brittle. Sharp bones can also puncture their digestive tract.

SHELLFISH - some dogs are ok with shellfish, but one of my dogs will vomit immediately, and this will happen with even small traces of shellfish such as prawns or langoustine. This doesn't mean dogs can't eat fish. They can eat fish, and fish is good for them in many cases. Always ensure it is cooked and sufficiently cooled.

XYLITOL (sweetener) and all foods containing Xylitol is toxic to dogs. It can cause your dog's blood sugar to drop and cause acute liver failure and even death. Early symptoms include vomiting, lethargy, and coordination problems or seizures.

Xylitol is used as a sweetener in several products including candy, gum, baked goods, diet foods, and even some peanut butter and toothpaste.

What to do if your pet is poisoned

These are the instructions from the Pet Poison Helpline:-

- Remove your pet from the area.
- Check to make sure your pet is safe: breathing and acting normally.
- Do NOT give any home antidotes.
- Do NOT induce vomiting without consulting a vet or Pet Poison Helpline.
- Call Your Vet or, in the US, the Pet Poison Helpline at 855-764-7661.
- If veterinary attention is necessary, contact your veterinarian or emergency veterinary clinic immediately.

The detailed instructions from the Pet Poison Helpline is as follows:

1. Immediately remove your pet from the area, and make sure no other pets (or kids!) are exposed to this area. Safely remove any remaining poisonous material from their reach.
2. Check to make sure your pet is breathing normally and acting fine otherwise.
3. Collect a sample of the material, along with the packaging, vial, or container, and save it – you will need all that information when you talk to your veterinarian or to a Pet Poison Helpline expert.
4. Do NOT give your dog any milk, food, salt, oil, or

any other home remedies! Also, never inducing vomiting without talking to your veterinarian or Pet Poison Helpline – it may actually be detrimental to induce vomiting.
5. Don't give hydrogen peroxide to your pet without checking with a vet or with Pet Poison Helpline first.
6. Get help. Program your veterinarian phone number, along with an ER vet and Pet Poison Helpline's phone number in your cell phone so you will always have immediate access to help.

Keep in mind that the prognosis is always better when a toxicity is reported immediately, so don't wait to see if your pet becomes symptomatic before calling for help. There is a narrow window of time when your puppy can be decontaminated (induced vomiting or pumping the stomach) in the case of a poisoning.

5

CHEWING AND MOUTHING

Puppies not only chew but there is a period when they will use their mouths - a lot! This is called mouthing, and their tiny teeth are remarkably sharp.

They will grab your trouser legs or put their mouth around your hands - and their sharp teeth will take your breath away.

Puppies need to learn about different textures - and human skin is just one of the textures they need to learn about. They also need to understand how hard they can close their jaws, and when enough is enough. They can only learn this by doing it. If you have children by very aware of this.

Mouthing

All puppies will go through this phase, and you will want to teach them about 'bite inhibition'.

This is something that puppies, who have come from a larger litter, will have learned a bit about, because they usually learn this through play with other puppies (and something early socialization classes can help too).

There were many times when Millie had her brood of seven

puppies, that we heard squeals of outrage or pain, as they pushed each other over and mouthed at ears, paws, and anything they could get their mouths around.

When one of the pups squealed, they would stop playing, but so did the protagonist. That pup tended to look as surprised as the pup that got a sharp tooth implanted into it. Yet, just a few moments later, they were back playing.

It was notable that the pup that got the painful nip was pretty eager to try this out on one of the other unsuspecting puppies.

This is just a part-and-parcel of a puppy growing up and learning boundaries. But it doesn't make it easier or any less painful. However, over time, all seven of the puppies seemed to understand each other and know how hard a bite they could get away with. The screams of surprise between them became less frequent.

Puppies are most likely to try and mouth you when you are playing with them, tickling their tummy, or petting them.

When Barney was mouthing, I decided to learn from the puppies and copy them only to discover that it is a common training method to deal with mouthing.

First of all - it's important to let your puppy mouth you.

Let him have your hand. When he closes his mouth too hard, and his sharp teeth become painful, squeal like a puppy or use the word "stop" and then stop playing with him. Just let your hand go limp so that it is no fun to play with.

This should stop your puppy for a moment or two. He will be just as surprised as you. When he relaxes his mouth and stops, then praise him. Then let him have your hand again.

He will definitely go too far quite a few times, so just keep repeating over a 15- or 20-minute time interval until he learns how hard he can close his mouth without hurting you.

If your squealing and "stop' doesn't work, then put him on

the "naughty step' so to speak. Stop playing with him for 30 seconds or so. After this, start playing with him again.

If he does it again, then repeat, and if this still doesn't work, then move away from him as soon as he mouths you and you feel that nip.

As the hard biting stops, you will want to continue teaching him as he moves his mouthing levels down from sore to moderate. Slowly teaching him not to mouth at all.

Eventually, he will know exactly the level of pressure that he can safely apply when he is playing.

Remember not to jerk your hands away from your puppy when he starts mouthing you. He still thinks this is a game and is more likely to lunge forward. Likewise, don't wave your hands in front of his face for the same reason—he will think it's a game.

Whatever you do, don't hit your puppy for mouthing. This will only make him play harder, but it may also cause him to fear you.

Once you have done this, you want him to learn not to mouth at all on human skin, and to let you pet them without being mouthed.

When your puppy tries to mouth you when you are petting them, distract him by giving him a treat or a chew toy. I ended up using a tug toy with Millie. I waved it in front of her and just said, "Play Tug."

This worked really well because she used to follow me around and grab my ankles to get me to play with her. To stop her doing this I would stand still and say, "play tug." It's classic distraction training!

When she stopped trying to grab my ankles, I would praise her. Eventually, I could walk around without being tailed by a puppy with sharp teeth.

One last thing to bear in mind. Like all toddlers, puppies

can have tantrums. His body will be stiffer, and his mouth might be tighter around the lips.

If you notice this while you are playing with him, just stop the play.

Don't squeal if he bites you (it will be harder than normal). If you are holding him, stop playing but continue to hold him for a few seconds, then let him go.

Don't make him afraid of you—you just want him to know that he has gone too far. If you notice that your puppy continues to have tantrums, you will need to get more help from a professional.

Chewing

Most dogs like to chew, and some breeds are more likely to chew than others. For example, Labradors and Staffordshire Bull Terriers tend to have a stronger desire to chew.

All puppies enjoy and need to chew. They do this to explore their environment and understand the texture of things; they don't have hands, and they like to pick things up. So the only way he can explore is to use his mouth.

Between the ages of around three and seven months, your puppy will also start to experience discomfort in his mouth as the teething process gets underway. He will chew to help remove his baby teeth, and he will chew to help with the pain of his adult teeth erupting in his gums.

As your puppy starts to reach adolescence, at around seven to 12 months, his chewing is going to get worse. There are two possible reasons for this.

It is around now that they tend to get easily bored so try to find new games (especially mental exercise games) and other games to keep them occupied.

It is also around this time that their adult teeth are settling into the jaw, which can be uncomfortable for some dogs.

Whatever the reason and it might be both of the above reasons, your puppy is going to chew at things.

In my case, it was furniture. This included the legs of tables, the sides of the sofa, shoes, wallets, and spectacles.

You will need to teach everyone in your household to put their shoes out of reach, and preferably out of sight, along with any toys that have different textures. These will be the favored chew items. Puppies love shoes—they are just about the right consistency of hard and soft making them perfect for exploring different textures. Much the same as furniture too.

Don't forget that your puppy might chew all of his life (mine stick to tennis balls now), but it will never be as bad as that first year. Dogs chew when they get older because it relaxes them and it's a calming activity (and they enjoy it).

Here are some chew toys and tips that might help.

- Try and change your dog's chew toys regularly by rotating them every few days. This will prevent him from getting bored and prevent him from looking for something else to chew that might look more interesting.
- Remove anything that you don't want him to chew and keep everything well out of reach. I lost a TV remote control and a pair of glasses by forgetting to move them to higher ground.
- If you find your puppy chewing on something that is not allowed, don't punish him or shout at him. This will only make him anxious. Instead, simply distract his attention and then direct him to a chew toy that you want him to play with. When he starts to play with it, make a fuss of him.
- Don't forget to remove anything dangerous to your puppy when he cannot be supervised. This includes

some types of household plants that are poisonous to dogs.
- Many hard plastic toys are not made for chewing by a dog. The best chew toys are made of the type of hard rubber that you get with your Kong. You can also consider activity balls (like Kong's, you can place kibble, cheese spread, peanut butter, or other treats or food inside). Ropes are also good but avoid nylon or anything that the dog can pull apart into a string.
- Chews such as dental chews or other edible chews can distract your puppy—they can be eaten quite quickly. These chews last just a few minutes with Barney, so I tend to use them less as a chew alternative. Some dogs can chew for quite some time on these, though. It is just a case of testing which chews your puppy likes the most.

6

RECALL TRAINING PREPARATION

You will need a few tools and some equipment to progress with recall training (and most other training). Here are the main items you will be using:-

Treats

Treats are the mainstay of dog training at the puppy stage, but try and introduce other rewards such as toys or praise too. In a few cases dogs can prefer toys to treats!

Some people cut up hot dogs, I made something called liver cake (it worked really well), and one of the simplest things to do is to grab a handful of his kibble and use this as a dog training treat.

Kibble isn't always seen by your dog as being of high value, so work out what his preferred treats are, and which ones he loves most.

You will then use this knowledge to reward based on difficulty, the more difficult the higher the reward value. It is important to use more than one treat so try and have a selection of 3 or 4 if you can.

This allows you to reward on value and, depending on what you want him to do, and how much he might not immediately understand or want to do it, you can use the treat that matches his effort.

For example, if he absolutely loves cheese then save this as a special treat when he does something for the first few times. If he has already learned to sit, then offer him kibble when he sits.

If he is doing recall and takes a long time to return then he gets kibble, if he returns quickly, he gets the cheese. This process can increase the connection between you and your puppy.

There are a few reasons that treats might not work. They might not be tasty enough, your puppy might not be hungry (try and train him on an empty stomach), he might be too stressed or he might get his treats all the time so he doesn't realize what the reward means.

Over reinforcement, which simply means using treats too often, is common.

This is why, over time, you will reduce the value of the treat as he learns the desired behavior, and why you will reward based on the quality of the response.

You are eventually aiming to have the desired behavior with no treats at all (you won't always be able to have a treat in your hand) but you will always praise your dog for returning to you and you may also have a reward game for him to play (a tug or a ball to throw).

The reward might not always be a treat and it doesn't need to be. A dog can never have too much love, praise or too much play.

Dogs train better when they are making their own choices, and you want him to want to make the choice to come to you, when you ask him. This means that you must never be angry when he comes back to you, no matter how long it has taken.

Harness

Collars and choke collars are no longer thought to be good for dogs. They can be worn in the house but harnesses should be used for training - especially leash and recall. Training is all about trust, and restrictive items just won't build the trust you are looking for.

If your puppy jumps around when you try to get the harness on him, a trick is to begin by holding a treat through the opening of his harness where you need his head to go and encourage him to put his head through to get to the treat. You need to deal with his legs so ask him to sit as you do this.

I use 'sit' and 'wait' as I pull the straps around his chest and under his legs. He usually stands (I just use the 'wait' cue for this part) for the lower strap. He just seems to find this more comfortable.

Reward each step and success and take it slowly.

Leash

Avoid flexible leashes. They won't give you the control that you need and they get tangled up in legs - all sorts of legs. You will ideally want to use a long-leash (around 25ft-30ft in length). This is known as a long-line.

You will also want a shorter training leash. His day-leash or 'normal' leash will be shorter than the training leash. A 4ft leash can work well as both a training and a day leash.

Whistles and Clickers

Almost all leash training will involve using a clicker - I train with and without a clicker. Whistles are great for recall especially for dog breeds that like to explore.

With clicker training, this must always be followed with a reward, for example, click-treat. This is known as the primary and secondary enforcer.

Eventually, you will click less and less as the behavior is established but you must always follow a click with a treat.

Toys

You are going to use your puppy's toys during the recall training. You are going to try to get him to leave a toy and come to you when he is called. You will have a treat so that he sees the value of leaving his toy and coming to get something else he loves.

If you are training a gun dog for retrieval then you can get lots of scent items such as rabbit scent balls and puppy dummies. We once trained a spaniel by scenting a sock with a pheasant and hiding it for them to find when asked to fetch.

~

Basic Training

In the first few weeks that your puppy is home, there is some basic training that you can start right away that can teach him some of the basic commands that you will use throughout his life.

Always keep the training sessions to between 5 and 10 minutes. If he comes up against something he can't do, then return to something that he can do, so that you can praise and reward him at the end of the training session.

I mention using hand signals during some of the basics described below, and you should try to use this type of training as much as your can, rather than just verbal cues.

Try your best to use both if you don't feel comfortable with only hand signals.

This is the same for using treats as rewards. Try to reward without a treat by using praise or other forms of reinforcement if you can.

Reinforcement (a part of operant conditioning) and using body language rather than verbal cues is now considered as the foundation for good dog training.

Getting to know his name

Always reward your puppy when he responds to his name.

It doesn't matter how or why he responds to his name; it only matters that he is, and that you need to reward him for doing so. This might be harder to do when he is chewing something that he shouldn't be.

Don't ever be tempted to use his name as punishment. He won't understand, and will be confused by your use of his name, and confused by your behavior and annoyance.

Look at Me

Before you start taking your puppy outside for walks you will want to teach him to look at you. To do this he needs to want to pay attention to you.

As an aside, this is great during training. If your puppy starts to get engrossed or fixated on something then get him to look at you - it changes his focus back to you. I find this particularly useful for leash training.

Simply reward him every time he looks at you, and repeat the process in many different locations and environments. You can reward him with click-treat, with praise and reward, and the reward might be some play or a toy (spaniels love a ball throw).

Training your puppy to look at you can be done with an easy game and it will teach your puppy to look at you, as well as getting him used to his name.

To play the game, sit down with your puppy with a handful of treats in your pocket. Make sure that you are sitting so that you are close to him, but that he needs to look up to see your eyes.

Take out a treat and get his attention. Place the treat between your eyes. Your puppy will follow the treat all the way to your head and eyes. As soon as there is eye-contact, even briefly, give him his treat.

In the beginning, the eye contact might be an accident on his part but that's okay. If he gets rewarded for it, he will soon learn. Keep repeating until he always has eye contact with you.

Keep doing this and then start putting the treat behind your head or neck but try and get eye contact before you give him his treat. If he doesn't look at you at first, then help him find your eyes so that he knows what he is supposed to do.

The next part of this game is to start using his name. Do exactly the same process but as you place the treat between your eyes, say his name. You will need to do all this quite quickly to link the eye contact ,and name call, with his reward but he will get there.

He now knows that when you say his name you want him to look at you, and he wants to pay attention to you, because there will be a reward coming!

Teach him to Sit

There are a few ways to teach your puppy to sit, but I have used this one to the best effect.

Sit down beside your puppy holding a treat, then put the treat in front of his nose, slowly lifting it above his head. As he tilts his head to follow the treat, he is likely to sit as he tries to reach the treat.

I would usually say the word 'sit' just before his bottom touches the ground. Then, as soon as his bottom touches the ground, reward him with the treat. Your puppy is learning the word sit but also starting to recognize your hand signal.

Keep doing this, eventually removing the treat from your hand but using your hand as a signal or cue to get him to sit, and saying the word 'sit' as you raise your hand to the sitting position. Always reward him as soon as he sits down.

The other way to teach him to sit seems to be something that kids are really good at teaching.

Just stand in front of your puppy with his treats and ask him to sit - holding a treat over his head. Then wait for him to sit, and as soon as he does, reward him with praise and a treat.

Next, move away from your position so that he needs to stand up, then repeat. After a few successful attempts, begin using the word 'sit' as he starts to get into position, rewarding him all the time. Don't try to push his bottom to the ground to get him to sit - it rarely works.

Teach him to Lie Down

For some reason, this is the fastest command to teach when you do it like this, and your puppy will be lying down within one training session.

Simply take out his treat and hold it to his nose, then move it down slowly to the floor (I usually say 'Lie Down' at this point too rather than wait until later in training). Slide the treat on the floor away from him if you need to. He will start to move down.

As soon as he is almost down (he won't lie down right away, and his bottom is likely to remain in mid-air), gave him the treat. Keep doing this and getting him to move further into the lie position (you can keep dragging the treat towards you on the floor as this can often help).

Reward and praise him each time. Eventually, you will only give him the treat when he is fully down. By now, he will be used to your hand moving down and hearing the phrase 'Lie Down.'

Teach him to stay or wait

You can use either term with your puppy. I use both, but in different circumstances. For example, I use 'wait' when we are crossing a road, and I want him to wait before I cue that it's ok to move.

On the other hand, I use 'stay' if someone comes to the door and I don't want him running into the hall. You can use the same command for both of these.

To teach your dog to stay, first of all, ask him to sit. Then hold up your hand so that your palm is straight in front of him and directed towards his face (but not in any kind of threatening way).

Take a step backward so that you are facing him with your palm facing him and say stay. If he stays for even a few seconds, come back to him and reward him.

Keep doing this while moving further away and then making him stay or wait for a little longer. Eventually you will start to walk away from him with your back to him, before turning around to face him, and returning to praise and reward him (you will complete this before adding the 'come' cue).

Leash training

You can start clipping on his lead in the house so that he gets used to it.

Recall training preparation

As soon as his leash is clipped on, give him a treat. Have a treat in your hand and use this to get him to walk beside you.

Hold it just in front of his nose, loosely cupped in your hand so that your palm is facing his nose with your arm hanging down beside you.

He will eventually be running beside you, or more precisely, running after your hand. Build this up slowly and for no more than 5 minutes at a time at the start.

Eventually, walk a few paces, then turn in the opposite direction getting him to follow you.

Repeat this process of walking a few steps and turning.

7

THE FOUNDATIONAL CUES

You are aiming to have your dog return to you on cue no matter how many other exciting things are going on around him.

This means that you want your puppy to want to return to you on cue, not only when there are no other dogs around, but also when there are dogs to play with.

You can only achieve this if you are more interesting than whatever else he is doing, and if he is listening, and paying attention to you.

In summary, you want him to stop what he is doing; you want him to look at you, and you want him to come to you on cue.

Like many things with training, it takes a little bit of time. Ideally, you want your dog to automatically return to you whenever he feels threatened. This means any bad situation can be avoided before it even begins.

Sit, stay is an important part of recall training and it's an important part of overall behavior. Ideally, every time he sees another dog, you will want to get him to come to you and sit and stay.

You will start the recall and 'sit stay' training at home, and you won't let him off leash outside in an unenclosed area until you are happy that he will return to you, and that he is already doing what you want him to do in the home or the garden.

To do this you, need to introduce different locations and then introduce lots of distractions as the training develops, because there will be lots of exciting activity and scents in the park, but wait until his recall is up to about 70%-80% before you start adding the distraction element of his recall training.

Decide on your cue

Most people use the word 'come' or 'here' as their vocal cue for their dog. Once you have decided on the word you want to use, then you must keep it. Consistency is vital for your dog to understand what you mean.

You will start using this early. When you want him to come for his dinner you will use it, when you are going to give him a big cuddle or play with him, you will use it.

The word itself doesn't mean anything to your dog, but the outcome of his action means he feels great and gets something he loves.

In training language, he is building a positive association with the word. Try to build in hand signals too - I tend to open my arms as a visual cue to come.

Like most training sessions, keep the training to around 10 minutes and watch out for any signs that he is getting stressed (quick head movements, grabbing the treat/food, ears flat) and try not to get over-excited.

If your puppy is a part of a household then get all members involved in the training too. At the end of his training get him to do something you know he can do so that it ends in success. You want him to enjoy his training.

Sit Stay and Release

Sit Stay is one of the most important cues your dog will learn. Dogs naturally want to follow you, especially as you move away from them.

You will want to use both verbal and visual cues. Your visual cue will be holding up your hand, but without raising your arm - just hold it in front of you and direct your palm to your puppy's face. This is his visual cue for stay.

The verbal cue would be 'Stay'. Visual cues are also a good way of helping your dog focus on you.

Normally the first part is to ask your puppy to 'sit' then this is followed by 'stay' (or 'wait').

By this stage (by the time you are going for outside walks) you will have trained your puppy to 'sit' and will have practiced some 'stay' in the home or garden.

To recap on the 'sit' training. Never force your puppy to sit by putting your hand on his lower back and pushing it down.

Decide on your visual signal for sit. An example would be to hold out your hand palm facing-up, then gently move your fingers upwards as if you are 'lifting' his head with your four fingers.

Take out a treat and bring it towards your puppy's nose slowly moving it up over his head so that he naturally goes into a sit position.

As soon as his bottom touches the ground praise him and give him the treat. If you are clicker training then use the clicker as his bottom touches the ground and provide the treat.

Try to make sure that you provide the praise/treat when he is sitting and not when he has moved to a standing position.

Whenever you see your puppy sit praise and reward him (with voice or clicker - click-treat) and then start introducing the verbal cue. You can start the verbal cue earlier, for example, say the cue 'sit' right before his bottom touches the ground and he is due to receive his praise/reward.

Every time after that, when your puppy sits try and remember to praise/reward them as this will build this into a behavior default. One that they enjoy and know brings praise/reward and they are comfortable and safe with.

You will want your puppy to sit for lots of reasons. In the car, when you go the door, at a crosswalk, and so on. This means you need to train him to sit but you also need to let him know when it's okay to move forward.

To do this, first of all, have him on his leash. Get him to sit (and reward) then decide on your cue for 'let's go' this can be 'let's go' or 'ok go' or whatever you choose. Say your cue and move a few steps and praise him, ask him to sit and reward.

Begin with short distances (a few steps) to get him used to the 'ok go' cue. Repeat the process of 'sit', reward 'ok go' reward, walk a few steps then repeat. This is known as the release command or release cue.

This can mean that the release cue is seen as a reward too because when he comes back he then gets to go and have fun again. It also means that he will learn that coming back doesn't mean the end of the play.

Finally, some trainers consider recall to include holding your puppy's collar when he returns as full recall and used before the release cue. The puppy comes back, he sits and the collar is taken then the reward is given. This is followed by the release cue.

Some are happy with only the sit. This really is up to you but I prefer the collar hold as it gives you more control should you ever need it.

8
RECALL TRAINING

You will begin teaching your puppy what you mean by the recall cue. I will use the example of 'come'. The important part is to always use this word and use it only when you want him to come to you. Don't mix it into other cues. This one word means one thing, and one thing only - to come to you.

You will adopt this rule for all his cues. Make sure each one is unique to the action expected and not mixed into other meanings or cues. For example, don't use 'come here' if 'here' is used as another cue.

Start your recall training in the house then move to enclosed areas with few distractions.

I know of someone who trained for recall in their hallway, which was ideal for ensuring their puppy was set up for success during the early training because there were limited directional options, and little distraction. This is important.

You want to ensure that your puppy always succeeds and this might mean you need to adapt things to make sure that he can succeed through each step of his training.

Get him used to coming to you

Once you have decided on your location, show your puppy his favorite treat or toy, and as he comes towards you to get his toy or treat (don't ask him to just let him do it by himself), praise him and reward him as he reaches you. Do this a few times.

After a few times start to add in his cue so that he gets used to it. As he starts coming towards you to get his toy (and ideally looks at you), add in the cue you have chosen. In my example, 'Come'.

Once he is doing this you can add in a sit.

As soon as he comes to you give him his treat and ask him to sit. When he sits give him another reward.

You then want to keep repeating this game in other rooms of the house and with more distractions.

One way to do this is to have other family members or friends in the room. As you walk towards them and he starts to get interested in this interesting and fun distraction, quickly run away and call him so that he chases you.

Encourage him to catch up and when he does, he will of course get his treat and probably a big cuddle as an extra reward.

Like many of the games you can play with him, mix them up so that he doesn't always know what to expect. It will keep him even more interested in what you are about to get up to next.

10 steps for basic recall

1. Decide on your location (hallway, kitchen, etc)
2. Show your puppy his favorite toy or a treat but don't call him, let him come to you
3. When he gets to you give him his reward.
4. Repeat

5. Start adding your recall cue as he starts coming towards you
6. Reward him when he gets to you
7. Repeat steps 5 and 6
8. When he comes to you give him his treat then ask him to sit and give him another treat
9. Repeat this until he knows what to do
10. Repeat the recall and sit training in other locations and start to add in distractions

Training sit-stay

Ask your puppy to sit, then 'stay' and still facing him, take a few steps backward holding up your hand in the 'stay' position. Walk back to your puppy and reward him.

Do this a few times and then take a few more steps backward increasing the distance then walk back to him and reward him. Keep repeating moving further away.

Your puppy is learning that not only is he getting rewarded but that you come back to him. Start to move to different positions so that you are to each side and eventually behind him. If he gets up, just move back to him and give him praise then try again.

You will need to repeat this in several different locations not only in one room or in your own garden. As he starts to get better at this begin to introduce him to areas with more distractions and start moving behind objects so that he can't see you. Try and do this everywhere you go.

Sit stay come

This was the main recall training I started with Millie indoors when she was around 14 weeks old and it was very effective.

Ask your puppy to sit and then asked her to stay as above (I used the word 'wait' and held my hand up).

Walk backward a few steps facing your puppy - I kept holding my hand up as I was walking away.

The difference now is that you want him to come to you following the sit-stay. If he stays for just a few seconds, ask him to come and give him a treat and be delighted with him.

Keep repeating this and do it at the start of every training session. As he starts to get good at this, start to move further and further away and eventually try walking away with your back to him.

Build up distance and distractions to this game - but if you go too far and he starts to come towards you too soon, just go back a few steps to the point at which it was working and then keep trying to build the distance.

The next stage is to go outside but not for a 'proper' walk just yet. You can go for a walk on-leash but not off-leash.

Going Outside - enclosed area

Training for recall outside of the house is vital. It is here where he is going to find the most distractions. You must make sure the area you choose in enclosed. Just like the early days of house training, you will start with very few distractions.

This is when you are going to work with the clicker and training leads and when you will start working out the value that he attaches to each of his different treats.

A great tip is to train your puppy before he has eaten - this means the treat you are offering will be of higher value to him and he will be more interested in them! And don't train him for too long. Pay attention if he looks like he is getting bored and stop the training and start again the next day.

You also want him to know that coming to you is more

rewarding than doing something else - it is exciting and fun and may involve a tasty treat.

I also used to crouch down and hold my arms wide as Barney ran to me when he was a puppy. It wasn't meant as a signal but even today if I hold my arms wide, he will come to me.

To get started, put your puppy in his harness and on his training leash. Just like the early indoor training, you can start with rewarding an action with no other cues, to get him used to the long-line and outdoor training. He will know what to do quickly, because he has already been trained indoors.

The difference now is that you are going to place something he might want to eat or go to, a short distance away from him, and within the length of the leash, or just a bit further away. You are now introducing something he wants to get to, that is away from you.

As he goes towards the object or the treat (but not too tasty), tighten his leash and say his name then the cue e.g., Barney 'come'. As soon as he turns and comes (only a step or two) reward and praise him.

If you are using a clicker, you will click as soon as he turns (there is more on clicker training later). Aim to have an even tastier treat for him than the one he was going towards. You want to increase the value of the treats the more you want him to do something, so that he prefers to choose that treat.

By having the leash on him, you can also gently encourage him to come towards you to get his reward if you need to. The leash helps you have a bit of control over this recall in the early stages as he learns the cue 'come' outside of the house, and where he will want to explore.

You will also play on the training leash and long line. Give him a few treats then run forward or backward a few steps and say 'Barney, Come!' in a playful voice. Hold the treat out at the height of his nose (so that all of his feet are on the ground) and as he reaches you give him his treat.

You can extend this game to add the sit. As he reaches you for his treat, move the treat up in front of his nose, so that he is forced back into a sit position to get his treat. In this way the come and sit are the same cue which means when you ask him to come, he will come to you and sit without being asked to sit.

You can, and should start practicing this as soon as you can. Puppies learn most up to the age of 18 weeks.

The next step for recall training is to have him move further away from you, and for him to return when he hears his cue. Good recall means he does this all the time. If he is not, then he is not ready, and you won't want to risk letting him off-leash.

To understand what you are asking your puppy to do, think about it like this. He is exploring and having fun, he is finding interesting and exciting things to sniff and play with.

When you call him, you want him to prefer to come to you rather than to do whatever he is doing. If you can achieve this, then there is no reason for him not to return to you when called.

To do this you will want to start with training games, and you will have worked out what his favorite treats are, and which ones top the list. Cheese, hotdog, carrot, kibble - my two dogs love cheese and I used the make liver cake which they absolutely loved. It was probably the single reason Millie's recall and leash training went so well.

Using the long-line

You don't need to use the long-line but it can be really helpful and, if you can, I would recommend it. To describe how this is done I picked a hand but you will end up doing something that works for you.

Practice this in a garden if you can, and, in the beginning, have no other distractions. You want to get used to working with the long line and you also want to test that your training is working.

Hold the end of the line in your right hand so that you have it tightly held. Wrap the length of the line into loops so that you can slowly release the line over the front of your body, feeding it through your left hand, making sure it can be easily released.

In your left hand, you are holding the part of the line that is acting as your dog leash, and it is attached to his harness, but your hand is operating as a feeder, controlling the delivery of the line.

This means you can slowly release the line through your left hand, to allow your puppy to move away from you, or clamp it closed (gently) to stop further release of the line.

You will have your right hand holding the end of the long line as well as the loops of the spare line.

Once you are comfortable you can start the training.

Slowly move in a circle on the same spot so that he is running around you, loosening the line so that he can move away from you, and then call him back to you. Just get him used to the leash and watching you, and knowing that he gets a reward when he comes back.

You can then add another game (and later you can play this off-leash too), by throwing a treat away from you, and letting your puppy go towards the treat.

Once he has eaten his treat, call his name to get his attention, and wait until he looks at you (click), 'come' (cue), and when he comes to you (praise/reward). Then throw another treat in a different direction so that he constantly running away and towards you in a fun game.

When you need to tighten or 'pull' the line to encourage him to come back on his cue, move or lean forward rather than move against him, and gently make the line shorter. This allows you to be in control of your puppy whilst letting him return without feeling 'pulled'.

The final part is to wait until he is preoccupied with something and is not looking at you. Get his attention and ask him to come.

If he comes then praise and reward. If he doesn't come, just walk to him and show him all the treats you have, and then walk away from him.

He is likely to follow you to try and get a treat. Just ignore him. As soon as he is not right beside you, ask him to come. When he does, give him lots of praise and a favorite treat. It won't take long for him to realize that coming is much better than not coming.

The next step is to repeat the indoor sit stay come training in the outdoor environment. Just as you did indoors get your puppy to sit-stay and then move away from him while still facing him and then ask him to 'come'. e.g., 'Barney, come'. Slowly build the distance all the while using the long line.

The next two steps are new, and before you can try off-leash outdoor you want to introduce the 'let's go' or 'let's play' cue which combines the sit-stay.

Ask him to sit-stay beside you, then use your release cue, 'let's go', and start walking. As he moves away and then moves ahead of you, call him back to you (click on a turn of the head towards you), as he starts coming towards you might want to encourage him (I held my arms open), reward him when he gets to you, then ask him to sit (reward).

The last step is to practice off-leash - again, you will do this in a space that is enclosed and where he will be safe. Simply let him wander away from you and then call him to you using your cue. Be exciting and have a treat ready for him. Try and keep his attention on you as he comes to you - make a noise or hold your arms open - you want him to be focused on you.

Don't keep repeating the cue or start raising your voice if he doesn't come. This will confuse him, and he won't be able to understand what his cue word is, eventually tuning it out which means he just won't hear it.

If you raise your voice, he won't think that coming to you is going to be lots of fun. Eventually, it could have the opposite effect, and he won't want to come at all.

The best way to train your puppy is using random and variable reinforcement. All this means is that over time change how often he gets a treat for the same behavior, so that he is hoping for it each time (don't wait too long to reward as you start to reduce the level of treats) and change the value of the treat (for a really good response).

If you want to, you can measure the average response time for recall (either daily or per 12 returns, etc.) so that when he comes back faster, he gets a super tasty treat. This is the most effective way to train your puppy to become addicted to coming back to you.

One last trick - if your puppy has taken a while to return on cue then, when he arrives, show him the treat and put it back in your pocket. As he moves away ask him to 'come' and, when he gets to you, give him his treat. This will help him learn that acting right away gets the reward.

Using a Clicker

Clicker training is useful when you want to mark the correct behavior of your puppy at the exact moment he starts to respond. As I have already mentioned, if you are doing click-reward then it must always be followed by a reward, but the reward and the timing of the reward varies.

In the beginning, all you need to do is get your puppy used to the click-reward (at the start you will use a treat). Keep repeating click-treat. He doesn't have to do anything at this stage as you are just getting him used to the clicker marker which means a reward is coming.

Slowly reduce the time between the click and the treat and vary the gaps - he will still expect the treat and he will know that it is coming, but that it might not happen right away.

Once he gets good at this, you will be able to click without the treat, and vary the reinforcement by using his favorite toy or a quick game that he likes.

For example, when you call his name and he begins to start coming towards you, you can click so that he knows a reward is coming. It helps to keep him motivated to come all the way back to you in the expectation of a good time when he gets there.

Recall Summary and where the Clicker fits in

The process for recall training is as follows:

1. Call your dog

Say "Barney", "Come" (cue - or use a whistle cue)

2. When he comes ask him to "Sit" (cue). Take his collar and praise him and reward

3. Release him "Ok Go" (cue)

If you are using a clicker as a marker then the full process would look like this:

1. Get your puppy to come to you

Start by throwing a treat away from you then throw a treat at your feet. Reward every time your puppy comes back to you for any reason. You can add the click with your clicker to mark as soon as he turns towards you.

2. Add a cue

As your puppy turns towards you, again, this is for any reason, add your recall cue and your click (if you are using a clicker to mark or capture the behavior). The recall cue can be 'come', 'here' or a whistle - either your own whistle or use a plastic one.

Practice at different locations and over different distances before you move to the next step.

3. As soon as your puppy looks towards you click and add the recall cue. As you are walking on the leash vary the length. Every time he looks towards you, click and then add the recall cue (and don't forget the reward).

4. You will now cue him to look and come to you. With your puppy walking in front of you say (or whistle) your cue, as he turns towards you add the click marker. Practice by varying the distance and the speed the dog is moving away.

5. If you want to add a sit then this is when you will add it to your training.

When he arrives back to you use your sit cue to get him to sit. As soon as he sits add a click and then the reward.

6. Add a collar hold. You can train this separately or you can add it into the recall process here.

When he has arrived back and sits, lean in and take hold of his collar - as you do this use your clicker to mark then reward.

Once he is good and is succeeding with steps 1 to 6 you can start adding in distractions.

You will start with low-level distractions and build them up to higher-value distractions.

Distractions might be kibble, bread, eggs, cheese, meat, and toys (again in order of least to most favorite).

As he moves towards the distraction e.g., the bread, start your recall with your recall cue, and the click-reward process above. If he fails then reduce the value of the distraction until he is succeeding.

In terms of what distractions might be, then this can be a dog he knows, a dog he doesn't know (high-value distraction), someone he knows, a group of people, a jogger, a bicycle an old scent, and the high-value new scent (a squirrel that you have noticed running up a tree).

Try and remember to complete a sequence. Try to always have your dog notice you (click), come to you (encouragement) arrive (treat), sit (treat), collar hold (treat), 'go play' (reward). This is much more rewarding than 'come', treat, end of the game.

By continuing to reward after he comes back to you, by rewarding the sit, collar hold and then releasing with a 'go play' cue, he will have the expectation of more exciting things to come than if the rewards ended with the return cue only.

He also knows that he can return to playing after if he comes back to you and receives all his rewards. Don't forget that the 'go play' cue is a reward in itself.

This will become even more useful once you start going outdoors to parks and other walks where there are even more exciting distractions and ones that you are not in control of.

Proofing

Proofing is when you want to prove to yourself that the training has worked. You will proof before you let your puppy off-leash.

To do this, you will create distractions and then aim to get him to come to you on cue.

You should also proof around other dogs. Try and arrange a play-date with at least one other dog and then while he is playing with them (and still on the long-line) call him to you. Make sure you have a very tasty treat and be full of praise when he comes to you.

Once he comes to you and receives his reward he is released to his cue, such as 'let's go', to play again. As already mentioned, this particular activity is also useful to teach him that coming to you doesn't mean the end of the playtime.

The last step is to practice off-leash - again, you will do this in a space that is enclosed and where he will be safe. Simply let him wander away from you and then call him to you using your cue. Be exciting and have a treat ready for him.

Don't keep repeating the cue if he doesn't come or start raising your voice. This will confuse him and he won't be able to understand what his cue word is. If you raise your voice, he won't think that coming to you is going to be lots of fun and, as noted earlier, it can lead to having the opposite effect and he won't want to come at all.

If he isn't coming to you as you go through all the training you have already completed go back to the long line until you are sure he understands what you are asking him to do.

Emergency stop

Training for an emergency stop can be one aspect of recall that saves your dog's life. It is also quite easy to train especially once you have been working on recall training.

First of all, you will want to use a specific cue. This can be any word but, again, it can only have one meaning. The most common word that is used is 'Stop'. Just make sure this is not used as a part of any other cue.

To begin with, have your puppy or dog sitting in front of you and have a treat in your hand. If your dog is not food orientated try using one of his toys.

Take a step back, put your arm in the air as if you are trying to stop the traffic or saying hello to someone who is a distance away. This is important as it is more likely that your emergency stop signal will be visual and not sound-based (call or whistle) when your dog is a distance away from you.

Raise your arm with the treat in your hand, say the word 'Stop', and then throw the treat over your dog's head towards his rear from your raised hand so that the treat falls behind him or just beside him. You want to make sure that your dog needs to turn around to get the treat.

As he starts to return to you, repeat by putting your arm in the air, saying Stop and throwing another treat over his head. This will force him to stop to turn around to get the treat.

You will notice that he starts to pay attention to you and your hand, which is what you want him to do.

Once he is paying attention, stopping and turning to get the treat as you raise your arm, you can think about increasing the distance. If there are any problems with the next step return to this first stage.

You will now start throwing the treat a bit further away so that there is a bigger distance between you so that when you say Stop, put your arm in the air, and throw the treat over his head, he is not close to you. This is how you can build up the long-distance emergency stop.

Try to make sure the treat doesn't land in front of him because you want him to turn around to get the treat. You want him to do this because it stops his forward movement. Keep building up the distance and repeating the exercise.

You want to reach the point where, with your arm in the air, you say Stop, he looks towards you and stops. If he starts to come towards you, go back to the first step and reinforce the stop when he is right in front of you.

If your dog is a fast learner it may take a few days but this can take a few weeks so just be patient.

The very last step is when you don't throw the treat at the end but instead, walk towards him to give him his reward. This is because, if you are in a park and he is far away you won't be able to throw a treat behind him. The final part of the training is letting him know a reward is coming.

What not to do

If your dog does not return to you when you call him simply go and retrieve him and put him on his leash. Don't be angry with him, simply put him on the leash, and move him away from whatever it is that is distracting him. This, in itself, lets him know that coming back is a much better option.

Don't keep calling the same cue over and over again. For example, if he does not come when you call and you keep repeating the cue louder and louder the cue itself will lose its value and your puppy will simply tune it out as noise. If your cue isn't working then choose a new one and train your puppy to know what it is.

Don't have only one person training him if he lives with other family members. If your puppy is a family dog then everyone needs to be involved in the training, and everyone needs to use the same cues. Ideally, everyone should be involved in the daily training, even for just a few minutes.

Never punish your puppy when he fails. This is particularly important with recall (and with separation anxiety). If you get angry with them, or punish them, when they finally return to you after not coming back right away, all he will learn is that coming back to you is not a good experience and that it has negative consequences. It is not fun. All this will do is make his recall worse, not better.

Don't use the "come" cue of your dog if fully focused on something else and is unlikely to hear you. In this case, use his name to get his attention and to check that he can hear you (does he react by turning slightly towards you or twitch his ear). If he does, then use his "come" cue. If he is far away you can use a whistle or whistle yourself, and if he can see you use your hand signal - in Barney's case this is wide open arms.

Only use your "come" cue if you think it is likely to succeed. If you call and he does not come, walk to him. Don't give him into trouble or reward him. If he does not 'come' you know he is not fully trained so re-start the training to the point he was succeeding, and build it up again from there.

Finally, do no use the recall cue for things they might not like doing. For example, don't associate it with a bath, or getting groomed, or having a tick removed. If you say the word bath to Millie she usually runs upstairs and hides, which is why I have used bath as an example. Some dogs love a bath! The main point is that you need your puppy to associate your recall cue "come", with something he is going to like.

9
GOING TO THE PARK

Once you are ready to move to the park where you will encounter even more distractions, you will want to begin with using high value (or higher value) treats than you have been using indoors and in the enclosed area.

It is going to be harder for him to return, and therefore you want the reward to be extra special. You will also vary these treats so he doesn't know what to expect but he knows a really tasty treat is coming.

You might also want to vary the timing of the treat so he knows it's coming and it will be tasty but it might be in 1, 2, or 5 seconds (you will want to start varying the immediacy of the reward when you are doing the outdoor enclosed training).

Try not to only call your dog to you at the end of his walk. If you do it throughout the walk and reward him each time he comes back, he won't associate recall with the end of playtime.

At the end of the walk, make coming back fun and rewarding rather than something he doesn't like. I tend to play more at the end of the walk as I return to the entry gate of the park.

During the walk, you can vary his treat reward depending on how well he comes back to you when you give him his recall cue. If you call, and he continues to do what he is doing for a minute or two and then comes back, don't reward him right away.

Let him smell his treat and then let him start to move away from you. Call him again quickly (you want him to be set up to succeed, he needs to know what you want him to), and if he immediately turns around and comes back then reward and praise him. He will then be able to learn exactly what you mean, and what you want from him, when you give him his recall cue.

In the early stages, try rewarding him with one of his less favorite treats rather than no reward at all for taking his time to come back. You want to ensure that he doesn't think he is being punished (by not getting his treat) for coming back, even if he took his time about it.

But remember, if you have already established a connection with your puppy and he finds you interesting, this will be much easier.

You can take your puppy to the park on a long line but never let him off-leash until you are confident of his recall. You can let go of the long leash and if he runs too far you can stand on the end of it. It is much easier to do this than try and grab a shorter lead.

As you start to venture out on walks, your puppy won't be the only one meeting other similar animals to talk and play with.

It's important to pay attention to your puppy and to keep playing with him, and being fun, during a walk too. Standing around and talking to other dog walkers and ignoring him will mean, although he might be well exercised through all his running around, he is learning that you are not the most exciting thing in his life and his attention to you (and your recall cue) may not be 'heard'. He will simply tune it out as his attention is elsewhere.

Other dogs and their communication signals

The first thing that is going to happen when you can take your puppy out for real walks after his required vaccinations, is that he is going to meet other dogs that you both don't know.

Your puppy is going to be playful and excited to meet other dogs, but these dogs may not be so eager to have an excited puppy trying to play with them.

Older dogs (those over 2 years old) are not likely to want to play - in fact - dogs over 2 years old will tend to only play with dogs they know. Many will stop playing with other dogs altogether. Both Millie and Barney don't play with other dogs anymore, they run along together or play with their balls or sticks.

You will also need to pay attention to how the dogs you meet are reacting. Dogs will tell you far in advance if they are getting annoyed, are uncomfortable or feel threatened. I don't know how many times I have seen the owner of a dog watch as his dog tries to get another dog to play, and the dog being approached tries, again and again, to say 'no' until eventually, it runs out of options and snaps or even tries to bite to the dog who is pestering it.

These are the general stages to watch out for, and this will be the case both for your dog, and for the dogs that you meet. Try to pay attention to what dogs are telling each other and telling us.

If a dog is displaying this behavior, then these are signs that he is feeling threatened, and is not happy with the attention of another dog, when it is close to him: -

Stage 1: Yawning, looking away, licking lips, moving away

Stage 2: Panting, hackles up, and whale eyes (when a dog shows the whites of his eyes). This is a clear warning signal. If this still doesn't work then the next part will be a lip curl or snarl

Stage 3: Lip curl or snarl or growl and possibly a snap. Then finally we will reach the stage we don't want to be

Stage 4: A lunge towards the other dog (or the source of the 'threat') with barking as your dog tries to make the threat go away and then this may be followed by a bite.

How dogs greet each other

You need to be aware of other dogs, and, when you meet them, watch and understand what they are saying.

A dog running at another dog is not going to go down well. I am still surprised how often I see dog owners letting their dogs do this. Both Millie and Barney are friendly dogs but they hate it. If you see a dog running towards your puppy or dog, then there are a few things you can do.

As soon as I see this happening, and depending on how far away the other dog is, and how fast they are running, I will throw a ball or a stick to distract Millie and Barney. This can sometimes encourage the other dog as well, and if I notice this, I just ignore the other dog and turn away with Millie and Barney in the opposite direction. If Barney is playing further away from me, and he feels threatened by another dog, he comes back to me to be safe. If a dog runs towards him, he comes as close as he can - he sometimes tries to jump up into my arms.

Millie tends to feel less threatened and seems to find it easier to deal with other dogs without resorting to aggression or fear. She must communicate well! She does this by a lip curl, then a growl, sometimes she adds in a whale eye, then an air snap but all of this is extremely unusual and she needs a lot of provocation. She always, like most dogs, starts with avoidance of the other dog if she can.

Others signs to watch out for include tails, are the tails up, and are the hackles up? Neither necessarily mean that the dog is aggressive but it indicates high adrenaline. If you notice this, distract your puppy or dog away from the other dog.

Two dogs that meet each other head-on and stare into each other's faces are not being friendly, but a dog that approaches from the side is being polite and asking for the intrusion into your dog's space.

A face greeting followed by a bottom sniff tends to be friendly. Bottom sniffing, generally, is fine and nothing to worry about.

If another dog puts his head across another dogs' shoulders this can be a sign of aggression and it can often be followed by mounting.

Just remember to always ask the other dog owner if it is ok for your puppy or dog to play with their dog. Do this especially if their dog is on a leash. Don't forget a dog that is on a leash might feel threatened by another dog, who is not on a leash, and who then tries to play with him. The dog on the leash will feel constrained, and this can lead to anxiety and a reaction to defend himself.

All of this is very important as your puppy begins his first walks. The experiences he has with other dogs at this stage are vital to how he views other dogs in the future, and if his experience is negative then he can easily build a negative association with other dogs - and be aggressive himself (he would see them as a threat).

One of the ways that you can help keep your puppy from getting over-excited around other dogs is to be more exciting yourself! Of course, you can also teach him sit-stay. Every time he sees another dog you will want to get him to sit and stay (and reward and praise him at each stage as he learns this). You can use a clicker if you wish, and every time he learns a little bit more, click and reward.

As you first start to take your puppy out, he is likely to want to run up to other dogs himself. This is very different as it will be clear to most dogs that he is not being aggressive but curious and playful.

However, and as noted earlier, dogs older than 2 years old don't tend to like being harassed by a puppy so just make sure you don't create a situation that then leads your puppy to start fearing other dogs. Millie, who is now 11 years old and has been a mum herself, will persevere with a puppy for a few minutes but she will then let it know to leave her alone. Barney (now 5 years old) will try to completely ignore a puppy for as long as he can.

However, puppies learn by meeting other dogs and learning not to bother them, so try and teach them the basics with a dog you know.

How to interact with humans

You will already know some of these but a couple of points are worth re-stating. Don't let a stranger pat your puppy or dog on the head. They can bring their hand slowly towards them from the side so he can sniff the hand.

If your puppy starts to back away this is a sign of fear, and an early communication, so try to notice it and don't ignore it.

If your puppy starts to yawn, or lick his lips, then this is the next level of communication, and he is really trying to tell you and the other person that he is uncomfortable.

The final warning will be a bark. He will only get to this stage if nothing else has worked.

The best way to try and teach him that someone is not to be feared is to reward your puppy when he sees them to create a positive association. You can also try showing your puppy that there is nothing to fear by touching, perhaps shaking a hand, and quietly talking, and while you are doing this, reward with a high-value treat.

Games

You will use games for lots of reasons. One of the things you want to get your puppy to do is to watch you, and know where you are. You always want to be moving around so that he knows he needs to keep an eye on you all the time.

Hide and go seek is also a great game to play. I love it more than the dogs and you probably will too.

This is a fun game that teaches them to pay attention to you. I still play hide and seek with them just to remind them to watch me and know where I am.

If you have forgotten how to play, hide behind a tree or a wall or any object. Let him run over to you and then come out, praise him and give him his treat.

A good way to play a game that reinforces paying attention to you (and can help remove any anxiety if other dogs are approaching) is to have them walk slightly in front of you and throw a really nice (and smelly) treat near you both for no apparent reason. This helps your puppy know that you might do something fun when he isn't expecting it.

A game I have found particularly good with my spaniels is ball play. They play with their ball all the time and always need to come back to have me throw it for them. It means when I am out with them, they rarely leave me. Barney, in particular, is obsessed with his ball - probably a bit too much.

Millie moves between balls, sticks and she loves pine cones (in the winter she loves to find a lost glove). They might surprise you with the things they love to retrieve (I call it 'fetch' and use this word as a cue). Frisbees are also popular and we had a retriever who loved a Frisbee.

Another great game is chase. As the name suggests, as your puppy is coming towards you give them lots of praise and get them to chase you. Most dogs love this game but some just don't have any interest in it, so this will depend on your own puppy. But changing up the reward, and keeping things exciting and different for your puppy is really important or they might get bored with you. Chase can also be done at any time.

Never play chase the other way around. Never chase your puppy or dog as a game. We see this a lot, especially on TV, because it's funny to watch but it really will mean your puppy just won't understand what you want. Chasing teaches him the opposite of what you want for recall (and being able to take hold of him, especially if you need to do it quickly). It will be very confusing for him when he doesn't get rewarded when he runs away from you. As cute as it can be, it can cause all sorts of problems.

Finally, and one last example of a fun game is piggy in the middle. This is a great game for recall and everyone can join in. As the name suggests, someone calls your puppy's name and gives them a treat or a toy, then someone else calls his name and he runs to them and gets a treat or the toy, and so on. This is actually great fun and a great way to get comfortable when you go to the park for the first time.

Your puppy will let you know what games and toys he likes best.

10

LEASH AND HEEL TRAINING

Leash training is a natural partner to recall training as most of the foundations are all the same and you will have read about most of them now.

For example, your puppy will need to know his name and you will also want to train your puppy to look at you outlined in the earlier chapters.

How to hold the leash

With your puppy on the left-hand side, hold the end of the leash in your right hand with the lead across the front of your body so that you are holding the other end of the leash in your left hand, with your hand closed over the leash, palm-side down. The treats will be in your right hand.

Ideally, start with your puppy in the sit position, and say 'let's go' or pat your side and start to walk. Control him with your left hand and say the cue 'close' or 'heel' while holding a treat in front of his nose just where you want him to be.

As you change direction use something to describe the

change such as 'this way' or 'change'. Don't use 'over here' if you are using the word 'here' in another cue.

To start this training, you can also simply put him on his leash and say nothing. It is likely that when you stand still and do this, that there will be tension on the leash. As soon as the tension releases click (if you are using a clicker) and place a treat beside your foot nearest to him. Just keep repeating as tension is created and released.

The only way to get a dog to stop pulling on a leash when you are walking is to teach the heel cue.

Walking to heel

Like recall, walking to heel on or off-leash is a part of daily life and therefore this training is vital. You will want to build it into his daily training routine and do it 2 or 3 times a day for 5-10 minutes.

Heel-work training is one of those times you want to make sure your puppy is hungry so that the treats can have maximum effect and reward. You might also find that you have to retrace the training slightly more often to ensure he is always successful.

Establish the heel position

The perfect heel position is to have your puppy's head or neck in line with the knee or leg. For ease, you can use his collar as a guide.

Like all training today, you are going to show him what you want him to do, and then you are going to teach him the word that describes what he is doing.

There are two ways you can do this that I have found work well and one shows on-leash and one shows off-leash.

1. Start with your puppy in front of you with the leash

around your right-hand wrist while controlling the leash with your left hand. Place your left hand about halfway down his leash towards his collar. Hold a treat in your right hand.

Get his attention by saying his name (or using a squeaky toy) and move your left leg back a step but remain stationary. Use the treat in your right hand to encourage him towards you and into the correct position and, as you do this, move your left leg back into position.

You will encourage him to move in a semi-circle to get into the correct position. As soon as he is in the position you want, mark with a click and a treat. You can then add the signal (I use a point signal) by holding the treat in the same hand that you are using to point down by your side. Once he understands this signal, add the verbal cue heel.

2. Start with your puppy in front of you with a treat in both hands. Hold out your hand and show him the treat in your right hand and then guide him around your back until he can see the other hand with a treat in it. It is this hand (your left had in this example), that will take him to the side of your leg and the final heel position. When he reaches the heel position praise him (or click) and give him his treat. Keep repeating until he understands the behavior.

Once you have done this a few times remove the treat from the hand that starts the movement (but keep doing the same routine) and keep the treat in the hand that guides him into the heel position. You will start to use the empty hand to create a visual cue such as pointing to the side (you can start doing this before you remove the treat).

After he has got the hang of this you can start introducing your verbal cue of 'heel'. Say 'heel' point and he should move behind you into the heel position to get his reward.

Start walking

One important tip with walking to heel is not to constantly hold the treat in front of your dog's nose. It will be tempting but it won't teach him what you need him to learn.

To build movement into his heel-work and walking, bring him to heel while stationary but don't give him the treat right away. Just bring him to heel, and then take a step forward so that he moves with you, and then reward him with his treat. Once he moves with you without hesitation move 2 steps and 3 steps and so on. Don't forget to give him lots of encouragement which will also make him want to look at you.

Every time he walks beside you in the correct position click and praise and reward and slowly build more time (and steps) between the reward. You are aiming to have him happily walking beside you in a straight line with only praise and lots of encouragement.

Once he is walking in a straight line you can then get used to changing direction. You can start to do this in lots of different ways but you can start by simply turning left or right.

Eventually, you will build in the other cues of 'this way' to change direction and his 'sit' cue. For example, you can ask him to sit after walking a few steps or before you change direction. Variations, as you move through his training, will keep him engaged especially as he starts to understand what you want him to do to get his reward.

Keep talking to your puppy and making lots of noises as you do this work - you want him to keep focused and interested in you. This will really help.

As you start walking with your puppy the leash should be relatively loose. If there is tension just stop and wait until the leash slackens then start to walk forward again. This will ensure that he can learn that there is only forward movement when the leash is slack. This works incredibly well.

Meeting other dogs while on the leash

When a dog is on a leash and he meets another dog the most likely meeting will be head-on and, as we already know, this behavior is rude in the world of dogs - and can even be seen as aggressive.

Being on a leash, by the nature of the leash-itself, makes this kind of meeting more likely, even if it is unintended by the dogs.

What you do, to try and avoid encountering this behavior, can unintentionally make things worse.

For example, if your dog is on a leash and he goes forward to another dog to say hello, and you pull him back and say 'no'.

1. This might start to create and build a negative association with other dogs.

2. If your puppy enthusiastically approaches another dog on the leash, this dog may not respond well even although they are normally friendly dogs. If this is the case, your puppy's association with other dogs might be that they are hostile and he won't understand that it was triggered by his over-enthusiastic approach. This means that he might start building a defensive reaction to other dogs.

How to greet other dogs on the leash

You need to train your puppy how to meet other dogs when they are on the leash and the best way to do this is to distract them from the other dog as they approach.

You will also want to get them used to greeting and meeting other dogs without making a fuss.

Start by training this with other dogs that he might know and then introduce dogs he doesn't know, but that that you know are friendly.

To do this with dogs that are coming towards you, use distraction until the other dog is near or has passed by. Just make sure that you are the one that gets your puppy's attention.

You are trying to get him used to other dogs approaching while on his leash without building any negative associations, and you are doing this by not allowing any situation to arise because he is focused on you, and not an approaching dog.

You will approach it like this whether he is on or off-leash but, when he is on the leash, he is going to feel more constrained and has fewer options in how he greets the oncoming dog.

The best way to do introduce your puppy to another dog while he is on the leash, and to educate him that he can do this as long as his leash is not being pulled, is to use direction change. As he starts to pull towards another dog, change direction by saying your direction change cue, for example, 'this way'.

This also releases the tension on the leash. Remember to reward him. Keep moving in the direction of the other dog. If you are a sailor this might remind you of tacking. When you get there ask him for a sit. Once he is sitting you can talk to the other owner and he can greet the other dog (just make sure you know the other dog is also happy to greet your puppy).

11

SEPARATION ANXIETY

It's important to understand separation anxiety because it should form a part of all puppy training.

Separation anxiety affects at least 1 in 7 dogs in the United States with some studies reporting it might be as high as 1 in 5. New Research from Finland has found that as many as 70% of our dogs are suffering from some kind of fear – and the most common is the fear of noise.

The very best thing you can do, if you have a new puppy or a newly adopted dog, is to train your pup as soon as you can.

Separation training is not generally top of the training list for new puppies - we all know sit, stay, leash and potty training and recall - but it is one of the most important training exercises that needs to be done to make sure you have a happy life with your dog, and one that teaches them that it is okay to be home alone.

Older dogs can, and do, develop separation anxiety, and this can be for several different reasons and it has happened to my dogs following the lockdown's of 2020 and 2021.

Separation Anxiety can be a form of separation distress or isolation distress - a milder form of separation anxiety. I use the terms separation anxiety as a general term but it will depend on the depth of the issue for your dog.

It happens when a dog reacts to separation (usually when their 'family' leaves the home) and this results in your dog getting stressed. This stress is released in a variety of ways, from whining and barking, to chewing and destruction, with a few poops in between.

This book is not intended for those dogs with serious anxiety problems, but rather as a guide, to help with some of the basic steps to ease your and your dog's anxiety with separation - and to also explain why they feel the way they do.

Dogs are used to living with others. They are pack animals, and in nature, are never alone. As mans best friend this means their pack includes us and everyone else we may live within our homes. In its simplest form, being 'separate' is not a natural experience for a dog.

Humans can, and do, live more separately. We are used to it because we need to do things like go to work, we might need to go to school or we just need to go shopping. We are therefore asking our dogs to behave unnaturally. This means that we need to teach them how to live in our world where some form of separation is a necessity.

Try to remember that for us our dogs, no matter how much we love them, are our pets. But, to them, we are a part of their pack. They see us as their family. They make no distinction between being human or not. And so it is natural for them to be with us and to follow us around - just like they would do with their pack.

There are a few theories on why dogs react the way that they do but the most important thing to know is that if they are suffering from any degree of separation anxiety then, for one reason or another, they are getting stressed when you leave and they are being left alone.

That is probably all that we need to acknowledge and then

all we need to do is to help teach them that being alone without you is not to be feared.

Not all dogs are the same

Separation or canine separation anxiety can affect all dogs. Although research suggests that dogs are more likely to develop separation behavior problems if they are male, come from a shelter, or are separated from the litter before they are 60 days old.

Interestingly, dogs born at home were more likely to suffer anxiety than those born with a breeder (this might explain why Barney, who was born at home. Is more anxious than his mother, Millie).

Separation anxiety can, and does, occur for other reasons. It also happens with puppy's and dogs beyond the puppy stage too.

Dogs that tend to have higher levels of alertness, which are more common in some types of breeds than others, are also thought to increase the chance of that dog experiencing separation anxiety.

In research, mixed breed dogs were more likely to destroy, urinate or defecate when left alone, whereas Wheaten Terriers were likely to vocalize, salivate or pant.

And where separation anxiety existed, almost all of the dogs also had a fear of noise. Miniature Schnauzers and Staffordshire Bull Terriers were the least affected by noise.

Not all dogs of the same breed will develop separation anxiety, it just means that there that they might be more susceptible.

Some examples of these breeds, in no particular order, are:-

Border Collies are not only highly alert but also very human-focused.

German and Australian Shepherds due to their high levels of vigilance, energy and loyalty.

Bichon Frises and Chihuahuas as companion dogs who love sitting around on your lap or getting carried around in your purse. They are used to being with you all the time.

Cocker Spaniels and King Charles Spaniels, just like the Labrador and Collie, Spaniels have been trained to work with us and strive to make us happy.

Causes and Signs Of Separation Anxiety

Separation anxiety is not a failure on the owner's part, and there can be many reasons that a dog reacts like this.

There may have been a change in ownership either from another home or from a shelter, there may have been a house move or a change in the routine of the family, it might be due to divorce or the loss of a family member (usually another dog but it could be a cat or even a family member moving away to school).

For puppy's, it might simply be the first time they have been left alone having been used to being around people all the time.

Dogs may also have had a bad experience - firecrackers, a delivery person, or the noise from trash pick-up. Dogs don't like sudden and unexpected noises.

Like anyone, dogs can get more nervous if they are alone. But remember, dogs are not used to dealing with threats alone, they are used to packs who are there for safety as well as nurture.

If they are already nervous or uncomfortable then they will feel even more vulnerable when they need to deal with these 'threats' alone in their home.

Finally, dogs may be bored. Boredom usually affects young

or energetic dogs who still don't know what to do when they are left to play - or relax - alone and they will seek out ways to keep themselves entertained. Like chewing furniture - this is also a calming activity - or exploring the trash. Exercise will help with this.

Dogs will do some of these things some of the time. But when they display this behavior some, or most of the time, then it is likely your dog is suffering from some degree of separation anxiety.

Dogs will get bored when they are left alone. Your dog will sleep – dogs sleep for between to 10 to 14 hours a day - but he will be awake at various points, and he will be looking for something to do.

He might have a sniff around, have a drink or two, and then look for something else to occupy his mind, his energy, and his time.

Dogs like to put things in their mouth, some things fit in their mouths and some things don't. This means that sometimes the mess you discover on returning home is simply a sign of a bored dog and not necessarily one suffering from anxiety.

This doesn't make the experience of returning home any more pleasant, but exercise will help, and finding toys that he can play with will relieve some of that boredom. Other signs, that are more likely to be separation anxiety, are more obvious.

The first thing I noticed was howling when I left the house. I didn't notice it - one of my neighbors told me that when the dog walker dropped them off after their walk they would howl for hours. Until this point, I had no idea.

This not only made me feel like a bad dog parent, but it also made me feel like a bad neighbor.

I would then leave the house for a few minutes and wait outside to see if this was an occasional thing or something they did all the time. Sure enough, after a few minutes, I would hear the howling.

This made it very hard for me to leave the house without worrying about them - and my neighbors. Commonly, the signs of distress manifest almost as soon as you leave the house.

Howling or barking is not the only sign of separation anxiety. Other signs are excessive barking, panting or whining, and indoor accidents. This won't be due to not being housebroken. Stress can result in either peeing or pooping or both. They may also chew things to calm themselves, scratch at doors or windows and some might try to escape.

They are more likely to be scratching the door that you left from, or the window from where they can see you leave, they might chew something that smells of you - a shoe, sock, or even a magazine.

Signs of general stress in dogs will be panting and pacing and this may well be evident in your dog if he or she is suffering from separation anxiety.

Is your dog panting when you return home? This might be due to whining and barking while you were gone. You will notice this at other times too.

Separation anxiety is not only when you leave the house and the dog is alone. It can also be when dogs become anxious when they are not seated near you or can't see you even if you are still at home.

Does your dog follow you around and want to sit beside you all the time? Do they sit against your legs or feet (this way they will know as soon as you move)?

What happens when you leave? Is it only you that your dog is focused on (if you share your home with family). In some cases, it doesn't matter if the dog is with another person in the home when you leave.

If you share your home and want to find this out, simply have a friend or another family member stay with your dog (with some treats) and leave the house. How does your dog react? Do they ignore the treats and look for you and if they do, how long for? Or do they settle down with the other person and enjoy their treats?

If you are not sure how your dog is reacting when you leave then it is useful to record your dog when you are not there. What does he do when you leave? Does he go to the door for a few minutes - how long? Take note of everything you can see and what he does. This is one of the best ways to find out what is happening when you are gone.

What to watch out for

Does your dog start to behave differently as you get ready to leave, either before you have started to get ready or when you are getting ready to leave? My dogs started to react to me picking up my coat or my car keys. If I was going on a trip - which might only be once every few months, one of my dogs would immediately start to pace around and look 'sad' as soon as I got a suitcase out.

The first thing to do is to take notice of their behavior and try and think about if it has changed and why it might have changed. What changes have you made, if any?

Notice how much and how often your dog is following you (even if he is a new puppy). If it's an older dog try to think back to any changes - is he sitting beside you more often, following your more than he used to? Is there any other reason or a point in time that you can identify?

The solution to this part of their behavior is to slowly build them up to being comfortable with you not being beside or near them so that they get used to your absence and learn (or re-learn) that you come back.

It is perfectly natural for dogs to show some anxiety - so don't over-react or worry about it. But if they do suffer from anxiety or nervousness, it is more likely they will also suffer from separation anxiety.

Sometimes any or some of the signs can be there for other reasons so if you are worried at all just check with your veterinarian.

Why Punishment Won't Work

Before we talk about all the things that can be done to help with separation anxiety, it is useful to understand why punishment just won't work.

Have you ever taken your dog over to the 'scene of the crime' and pointed at it? I have done this and we all will have done this.

Notice that the dog appears to look guilty and might cower. We, as humans, project our feelings or interpretation onto this behavior, and assume that the dog is noticing what it has done and feels 'guilty' about it.

This is not what is happening. What we see as 'looking guilty' is appeasement behavior. It can be a way that your dog is releasing tension to try and get rid of their fear. The cowering, flat ears and tail between the legs, or looking away, is your dog trying to placate you.

The dog will know that she emptied the trash all over the kitchen floor and dragged some of it into other rooms, but it won't connect what it has done wrong.

And he definitely won't connect something that happened 2 or 3 hours ago when you arrive home to find the mess.

All your dog will know is that you are not happy and he will pick this up from you and be fearful, and will try to placate you but he won't know what he has done. He only knows that you are unhappy right now. No matter how much you point at that mess your dog is not going know why you are angry.

Dogs won't associate something done hours or even minutes ago with the here-and-now. No matter how much we tell them, they simply won't understand why we are angry with them - just that we are.

And this means they won't understand why they are being punished. They will only connect that you arrive home and they get punished.

This all means that punishment when you return home will make your dog not only stressed about you leaving, but stressed about you coming home too. This can make any anxiety worse.

Just remember, the dog has not done this to deliberately annoy you nor to 'get back' at you. Dogs just don't think like that. They did it because they were stressed and anxious or bored and they tried to use that pent-up energy.

They might look 'guilty' when you return because they have learned that they got into trouble the last time you came back - so they appease you as soon as you return.

But they are doing this because when you return, they sometimes get punished, so they react to prevent it as much as they can.

Preparation and Socialization

It's a good idea to get your puppy used to being separated from you when they are young. Even if you don't expect to be away from them often, there will be times when you will need to.

Teaching your puppy not to fear this absence, and to let them know that they can be relaxed when you are not there, is one of the best things you can do for both your puppy, and for yourself.

If your puppy can get used to being left for short periods when they are young, then they are more likely to grow up feeling relaxed and comfortable when left on their own for part of the day.

These are all really simple things to do and are obvious

once you know them. You will need to do this slowly, teaching them bit by bit over time.

The first 3 basic steps you need to take are the following ones.

1. Pick the room you want your puppy or dog to be in when you are not in the house - either in their basket, bed, or crate. Decide which room this is going to be as early as you can.

2. Once you decide on where this is, start getting them used to being in this room - don't wait until the time when you are going to leave the house.

3. Spend time with your puppy or dog in this room - you want them to understand it is not a punishment 'place' or a place that is apart from you, but a part of their household.

Create a physical barrier between the room you want them to remain in, and the room you are in - make this something they can see you through (like a gate).

Once you have picked the room that you want your dog to stay in when you leave the house, create a gate to the room but make it a barrier or gate so that your dog can still see you. Remember not to interact with your puppy or dog when they are there - just go about doing things as normal.

Don't forget to spend time with them in this room when you are **not** about to leave, spend time there during the day, or when you are training them so that this becomes a place that you are a part of too.

As you begin their training, the first thing you will do after you have created the gate, is to just be on the other side of the gate to your dog. Do this for 2 or 3 minutes but, if your dog starts to get stressed, just calmly let them out.

Keep building their confidence and slowly make the time longer. Start moving around and doing other things as you build up the time and distance. At this point, you will always be in sight.

If they start to get anxious just move forward or return to

the point where they were comfortable. Once they are comfortable with the distance, start to move out of sight to another room for a few minutes, and then repeat the process of stretching the time. Begin by moving to the door of the room.

Then move into another room out of sight (but they will still be able to hear and smell you). Return after a few minutes, and then repeat building up the time as you go along.

Finally, go to the main door and go outside for a few minutes. Once again, repeat the process of increasing the time you are away and check how your dog is reacting.

If there are signs of stress or anxiety just go back a couple of steps and begin building up your dog's confidence once again. Keep the time as short as you need to, it can start with as little as 5 or 10 seconds, and build the time based on your dog's response.

From the very start let the dog know that the place you have chosen is their safe place. Keep all their things in this room and place their bed or crate in here as soon as you can, along with some toys.

If you are using a crate, keep the crate door open - let them get used to going in and out of the crate and choosing to do so.

Get some chew toys for them. Chew toys are good because chewing is calming action (and it's why they chew things they shouldn't). You could also put an item of your clothing in the room so that they can more easily smell you and feel more secure.

The chew toys help your dog use their mind to try and work out how to get the food or treat removed. Giving a reason for dogs to exercise their mind keeps them busy and happily occupied. A Kong is a great chew toy to use because, as well as the chewing, the fun of getting the treats or food out of the inside of the Kong exercises their mind.

Put on some sound - like a radio talk station. Not at a high volume - you only want to muffle any unexpected sounds.

This helps my dogs. I use either the television news or channel that is not likely to have shows with sudden noise but a talk radio station is probably better. Whatever you choose make it something that you listen to so that they are familiar with it.

Your dog will be paying attention to any noise they hear, so this can help disguise some of the day-to-day noises that might go on outside (or inside) your home. It is useful to do this as soon as you begin the training so that it becomes familiar.

Try to teach your dog not to follow you all the time in the home and get them to go to different places in the house. Test them being in a room while you are in another. Don't force this or make them feel stressed about it. You need to teach them to be comfortable with it.

Play a game where you ask them to remain in one room while you move to another, then come back. If they stay where they were, come back and give them a reward - it can be a treat or affection/well done. Once again, do this calmly because if you do, then you will keep your dog calm too.

Remember, when you come back not to increase or cause excitement. This can be a great game for your dog and they will enjoy it as much as you enjoy the results of it.

When you are ready to start the next phase of actually leaving the house there a few more things you can do to keep your dog calm while you are out.

How to leave and return

Start by leaving the house for a minute, 2 minutes, 3 minutes, and so on, and try and return before they are anxious. If you can, then leave for longer and build up to an hour and so on. If you notice they are not comfortable, then go back to the point when they were, and start from there again. Build the time up again.

Aim to build the routine - perhaps a treat as you leave. But don't kiss and cuddle them and make a fuss with gestures and by your comments. Try and make it as normal and calm as possible.

Of everything I did to help with Barney's separation anxiety, this was the single and most effective technique. It seems so simple yet it seemed to (and still does) calm him. I stopped saying goodbye or paying attention when I left. I just put on my coat, made no fuss at all, and left calmly.

Once you start leaving altogether, do so for short periods at the start if you can, and build up the time to 2, 3 and 4 hours. Do everything as normal and as they are now used to - and make sure they have something to play with or to eat.

Ideally, don't leave your dog alone for more than 4 hours. If you can ask a neighbor or a friend to visit - one your dog might know - or a dog walker. If you are able, come home from work for lunch.

You might start to notice that your dog starts to get anxious when you put on your shoes or coat or if you pick up keys or a bag.

If they start to react to these signs then start training them to get used to these things. Put on your shoes or coat or grab your keys but don't leave. Do something else or sit down and relax (or watch the TV). Keep doing this during the day so that they don't associate these things with your departure.

For example, one of my dogs would start jumping around as soon as I got my boots out. Initially, I put them on in another room, and then I realized I had to be in control of their reaction. I put the boots on then didn't leave (you can do this with keys/coats etc, pick them up or put it on and just sit for a while).

You can also try body-blocking. I used this with the younger dog, Barney (he was more excitable). As soon as he started to get agitated as the boots or coat came out I interrupted his behavior by standing up straight and then asking him to go to his basket. It's important not to be angry - they aren't doing anything wrong - you just want them to do something else so let them know what that is e.g. go to their crate or their basket.

You might need to re-trace your steps a few times, and go back a few paces in the separation training from time-to-time, as you are building their confidence and their sense of 'normal'. Just go back to the point where your dog was last comfortable.

Take this slowly - leave and come back. Build their knowledge and confidence. Having them exercised will help reduce their energy levels so remember to make sure they have had a walk and have been fed. This will make them tired.

You can also try giving them a favorite treat. This might help them associate your departure with something they can look forward to. Someone I know uses a hollowed-out bone with frozen dog food inside (they put the dog food in the bone then freeze it). You could do the same with a Kong.

When you return, don't get them excited with happy cries of "Hello!". Don't over-excite them, or over-reward them when you come back. Just arrive home and then ignore them for 5 minutes. You need to make the exit and return a very normal thing rather than any kind of event to be excited about.

If they have done something wrong on your return don't punish them or shout at them. They won't understand why.

Summary

- Don't make a fuss of your dog when you leave. Don't kiss them and say 'goodbye'.
- Leave calmly.
- Give them their favorite treat as you leave - give them something to chew on.
- Make sure they have been exercised.
- Don't excite them as soon as you return home, wait a few minutes before greeting them.

(These steps were the most effective things that I did to help my dog with separation).

Leaving when using a crate

When you put your dog in their crate (if you use a crate) before you leave then don't close the door right away. Put them in and wait until they calm down or lie down.

This might take a few minutes or more so do something else and give them time to relax and be calm. Close and open the door a few times if you like, but wait until they lie down before you close the door.

Don't bribe them into the crate with a treat and then immediately shut the door - just take your time, and let them take their time to get comfortable.

Once they are comfortable in their space and their room then you can start moving away using the methods detailed in the first step.

Some other useful tips

1. Exercise is an important part of curing separation anxiety.

A 2015 study by PLoS One found that dogs with noise sensitivity and separation anxiety had less daily exercise.

This suggests that exercise is one of the biggest things you can do to prevent or improve separation anxiety in your dog.

You need to make sure your pet gets lots of exercise every day because a tired, happy dog will be less stressed when you leave.

The study also found that dogs that were exercised off-leash were less likely to suffer from separation anxiety or fear around noise. The likely reason for this is that being on a leash, partly on a leash, or running free, has an impact on the amount of exercise a dog has.

2. A dog whines when it starts to get tense or excited - think of as them releasing their energy. Sometimes they whine because they want something - if this is the case, they will make it obvious what they want. If you notice this and the reason is not obvious then try and work out why it might be excited and calm them down before the excitement level rises.

3. If you have multiple household members - try and share the dog equally amongst everyone - so the dog doesn't focus all their attention onto one person. If there are more members then one can leave and he dog will worry less. Research shows that dogs in multiple person households are more likely to suffer from separation anxiety - I had expected it to be the other way around.

The 10 Steps to help Separation Anxiety

1. Create a physical barrier between the room you want them to remain in and the room you are in - make this something they can see you through.
2. Put their bedding or basket in this room along with any of their toys and the bowls.
3. Put on some sound - like a radio talk station. Not at a high volume - you only want to muffle any unexpected sounds.
4. Teach your dog not to follow you all the time in the home.
5. Don't make a fuss of your dog when you leave. Don't cuddle and kiss them and say 'goodbye'
6. Leave calmly
7. Give them their favorite treat as you leave - give them something to chew on
8. Make sure they have been exercised
9. When you return don't over-excite your dog as soon

as you arrive home (if there is a mess, don't punish your dog)
10. Wait a few minutes before you acknowledge them and say hello.

12

WHAT BREED IS RIGHT FOR YOU?

I have outlined some examples of dog types in this chapter that provides a brief and general overview. Please remember that these are general traits of the breeds, and that not all dogs will behave as predicted by their breed heritage. Take your time deciding on the type of dog you would like, and consider your family life, and your lifestyle.

Some dog breeds are great with children, while others prefer a quieter life. Some dogs need lots of exercise, and others need hardly any at all. Do you want to hold your dog and have your dog on your lap? Do you prefer a male or female dog (I have one of both), and what are the differences, if any?

GROUPS OF DOG TYPES

Dogs are generally split into seven types, and these are:

Sporting

Gun dogs are working dogs and were bred to accompany their owner. They are loyal and are good at retrieving. They were bred to either disturb birds or to bring them back to their owner.

Examples include Spaniels. I have two spaniels, and they are good at retrieving (playing fetch), but they never bother chasing birds or are even remotely interested in them. I know of another spaniel (the grandmother of Barney) who will jump into a lake and swim across it to follow a bird! It just means that there are no hard and fast rules. They tend to be energetic and need exercise.

Other examples include Retrievers - bred to retrieve the game and bring it back to the owner without damaging the game in their delicate mouth. I grew up with a retriever, fantastic with children and terrible at 'fetch' but loved to have a stick thrown. He was a beautiful, gentle giant called Paddy.

Other gun dog types are Pointers and Setters, and they were used to find the game and then point it out (as the name Pointer suggests).

The Sporting Group includes the American Water Spaniel, Chesapeake Bay Retriever, Cocker Spaniel, English Cocker, Curly and Flat Coat Retriever, English Setter, English, and Welsh Springer Spaniel, Pointer (German Shorthaired and German Wirehaired), Golden Retriever, Golden Setter, Irish Setter, Labrador Retriever, and the Weimaraner.

Hounds

Hound dogs fall into two types - sight hounds and scent hounds. As you would expect, sighthounds hunt what they see, and scent hounds hunt by using their nose. They all like to hunt as a pack.

Hound dogs, as a group, can be stubborn and very independent. They love to use their mind but don't always respond to commands. If you can keep them mentally active, then this will help. However, they are also more likely to wander off, so you need to keep an eye on them.

Scent hounds include the Basset Hound, the Beagle, and the Dachshund. They have the most sensitive noses of all dog breeds, and they love the sound of their voice. They would use this to let the leader know that they are following a scent, but they tend to use their voice (bark more) even if they are not used for hunting.

Some hounds produce a unique sound known as baying. If you don't know what this sounds like, check it out before deciding to get one.

The Greyhound is famously lazy if you want a dog low on energy, especially when they get older. It's amazing to think that they are racing dogs yet would prefer to laze around all day.

Examples of Sighthounds include the Afghan, the Greyhound, the Irish Wolfhound, and the Whippet. Although these hounds move at speed, they also love to relax. They will happily spend the day relaxing in their older years, requiring little exercise compared to other dog types.

Herding Dogs

As the name suggests, herding dogs were bred to herd and great at herding small children too! They are very loyal and are great family pets. These are very intelligent dogs and need lots of mental stimulation and exercise; otherwise, they might create it themselves. Examples of Herding dogs include the Border Collie and German and Australian Shepherds. Some, including the German Shepherd, can suffer from separation anxiety.

If you are also looking for a guard dog, the German Shepherd is thought to be the best. He is great for families with children, but you will need to train them well and find good training courses. If you do, they will be incredibly obedient. They will need a lot of exercise so bear that in mind too.

Remember that there are different types of German Shepherd too, some are better as family dogs and some better as guard dogs. These dogs are very intelligent and deserve to be well trained. My personal favorite as a family dog is the White Shepherd.

Working Dogs

Working dogs have been bred for their strength and are usually larger dogs. They have worked with us for a long, long time, either pulling sleds, performing rescues, or guarding our property. They are very intelligent and are great companions. However, due to their size and exercise requirements, they tend not to be ideal for families.

Examples of Working Dogs include the Akita, Bernese Mountain Dog, Boxer, Bull Mastiff, Chinook, Doberman Pinscher, Giant Schnauzer, Newfoundland, Rottweiler, Saint Bernard, and the Siberian Husky.

The Siberian Husky falls in the sub-category of pulling dogs. As the name suggests, pulling dogs (also the Alaskan Malamute) are used to 'pulling,' and they will need a great deal of exercise. They don't tend to make great pets because of this, but if you decide on this breed, remember to get a strong harness as they are very powerful, and you may find yourself getting taken for a walk rather than the other way around.

Terriers

The name terrier literally means 'dog of the earth.' They were bred as farm dogs. They chased and found foxes and other vermin. Because of this, they tend to explore holes in the ground, no matter how small.

They are full of mischief, are usually excitable, and are full of energy. They make great pets, but you will need to put up with their mischief and feisty personalities. They tend not to like other dogs, and their wiry coats may require special grooming.

Examples of Terriers include Jack Russell, the Scottish Terrier, the Patterdale, the Cairn Terrier, the Border Terrier, and the West Highland Terrier.

Toy Dogs

Toy dogs, or lap dogs, were bred as companions, and they adore affection and lots of petting. They have lots of energy and are very playful. They also don't tend to shed their coat, so they are ideal if you have an allergy or want to avoid grooming.

These dogs can become very attached to one person and are prone to separation anxiety, so try to consider them and train them to cope with separation. Some of them don't like noise and can be prone to barking (the Chihuahua).

Examples of this breed include the Bichon Frise, King Charles Spaniel, Chihuahua, the Maltese, the Miniature Bull Terrier, the Pekingese, Pomeranian, Pug, Shih Tzu, and the Toy Poodle.

Non-Sporting

Non-sporting dogs are dogs that do not easily fit into any other group. They are all very different in terms of size, coat, and personality.

The breeds in this group include the American Eskimo, Bichon Frise, Boston Terrier, Bulldog, Chow Chow, Dalmatian,

Keeshond, Lhasa Apso, Miniature Schnauzer, Poodle, and the Tibetan Spaniel and Terrier.

Lifestyle considerations

Do you have an allergy?

If you are prone to allergies, you are looking for a dog with short coats and those that tend not to shed. Toy dogs and Terriers would fit this profile. Poodles, for example, don't shed any hair. Other low-shedding breeds include the Schnauzer, Bichon Frise, Shih Tzu, and the Yorkshire Terrier.

German Shepherds, on the other hand, are often referred to as German Shedders by their owners. They shed a lot of hair!

Do you have children?

The Labrador Retrievers are well known for their loving nature and being good as part of a family. Other breeds that are great with children include the Newfoundland, Boxer, English Bulldog, and Irish Setter (as examples).

Do you have time for lots of exercise?

If you live in an apartment or don't want to or cannot commit to lots of exercise, you are most likely to be considering a low-energy dog. Toy dogs and some types of hound, e.g., a Greyhound. The Greyhound is one of the world's laziest dogs. Remember that low-energy dogs are not necessarily small dogs.

High energy dogs include the Airedale Terrier, Australian and German Shepherd, Border Collie, English Springer Spaniel, Miniature Pinscher, Pointer, Siberian Husky, Staffordshire Bull Terrier, Weimaraner.

How strong are you?

If you are not strong, then try to avoid working and some herding dogs if you can.

Do you have neighbors nearby?

Avoid the dog that is prone to barking more. For example, the Scent hound group - Beagles, Bassets, and also Schnauzers.

13

CONCLUSION

The first few weeks of having your puppy at home are both exciting and scary. However, once you can get your puppy used to his crate and going outside to pee or poop, then two of the most important aspects of his training, and living with you, will be completed.

Both of these will mean that your puppy can go anywhere with you but that he will also feel safe and secure when he has to stay at home when you go out.

You will worry about other things once he is home, and I hope I have covered most of them in this book.

For example, feeding and when to provide food is something I had to figure out when the puppies were little. I had never really considered what toys might be best until I had to decide which ones to get.

You will soon forget all the annoying little aspects of the first early weeks when your puppy will do some very annoying things —the mouthing and chewing are maddening at the time and the house training can be annoying as well as a little messy.

I would encourage you to train recall as soon as you can.

This is training that can save his life, as well as enabling you to love your walks together.

Recall training encapsulates almost every element of training your puppy will need other than potty and crate training. As well as bringing in all the cues, such as sit and stay, and the recall cues of come and heel (for walking beside you), it keeps your puppy, and later your dog, safe.

Some of the training steps might take longer than others but try to do them and complete them at the pace that works for your puppy. Just remember that our words mean nothing to a dog, and we are teaching them both a word and an action that we want them to do. And don't forget your visual cues.

Don't give up. As you see your puppy progressing, try not to settle for good enough. I have done this too. Barney was good enough and this was the case for his first few years, but as he got older, he became bolder and more confident, and this is when I wished he knew his recall better. It wasn't until then that good enough was really not good enough.

Good recall means that you and your dog can spend many happy hours together in parks, on beaches, in forests, and in hills and places you need to go.

It means he can share as much of your life as he can, and you will never worry about him being safe. Just don't forget to always keep an eye out for him, sometimes he won't be aware of dangers that he can't know about or see and for recall to work we need to use it, and to be able to use it when it matters most.

Of all the things I have learned over the years, the one crucial bit of advice is to remember that your puppy and your dog only want to make you (and himself) happy. So don't punish him when he gets things wrong; he is doing his best.

Just teach him what you want him to do and let him know he is on the right track by using rewards, treats and love.

All dogs are different and some breeds will find different aspects of the training harder. If you are getting frustrated or stuck then take your dog to training classes or to a trainer. These training sessions can be invaluable and will sort out what you are doing wrong quickly.

And try not to get him over-excited when you leave or return home. It really is the best way to train your puppy and prevent anxiety—and it works.

14

NEED MORE HELP?

I just came across this fantastic (and free) online workshop on training your dog to become as well-behaved as a service dog.

I loved the workshop so much that I wanted to share it with you immediately.

Check out the free workshop here

The workshop is designed to help "normal" dogs like yours have the same level of calmness, obedience and impulse control as service dogs.

It's being conducted by Dr. Alexa Diaz (one of the top service dog trainers in the U.S.) and Eric Presnall (host of the hit Animal Planet TV show "Who Let the Dogs Out").

Frankly, the techniques described in the workshop are fairly groundbreaking - I haven't seen anyone else talk of these techniques.

This is because it's the first time ever (at least that I know of) that anyone has revealed the techniques used by the service dog training industry to train service dogs.

And more importantly, how any "regular" dog owner can

apply the same techniques to train their own dogs to become as well-trained as service dogs.

It's not a live workshop - rather, it's a pre-recorded workshop, which means that you can watch it at your convenience.

However, while the workshop is free, I am not sure whether it's going to be online for too long, so please check it out as soon as you can.

Here's the link again.

OR YOU CAN USE this QR code.

15
LEAVE REVIEW

As an independent publisher with a small marketing budget, reviews are my livelihood on this platform. If you enjoyed this book, I'd really appreciate it if you leave your honest feedback. You can do this by clicking the link to leave a review. I love hearing from my readers, and I personally read every single review.

RESOURCES

Alt, K. (2020, August 14). *Am I Ready For A Dog? How To Be A Responsible Dog Owner.* Canine Journal. https://www.caninejournal.com/am-i-ready-for-a-dog

Animal Poison Control. (n.d.). The American Society for the Prevention of Cruelty to Animals® (ASPCA®). https://www.aspca.org/pet-care/animal-poison-control/people-foods-avoid-feeding-your-pets

Answer These 5 Questions to Find the Right Dog For You. (2017, November 2). American Kennel Club. https://www.akc.org/expert-advice/lifestyle/answer-5-questions-find-right-dog/

Blue Cross For Pets. (n.d.). Blue Cross For Pets. https://www.bluecross.org.uk/advice/dog

Committee on Nutrient Requirements of Dogs and Cats. (2006). Your Dog's Nutritional Needs. Retrieved. (2006). Https://Www.Nap.Edu. https://www.nap.edu/resource/10668/dog_nutrition_final_fix.pdf

What Size Dog Crate Do You Need? (n.d.). Cooper's Crates (www.Cooperscrates.Com). https://cooperscrates.com/pages/selecting-the-correct-kennel-size

Your Complete Guide to First-Year Puppy Vaccinations. (2021,

February 5). American Kennel Club (Www.Akc.Org). https://www.akc.org/expert-advice/health/puppy-shots-complete-guide

Gibeault, MSc, CPDT, S. (2021, February 3). *How To Teach Your Dog To Sit.* Https://Www.Akc.Org/. https://www.akc.org/expert-advice/training/how-to-teach-your-dog-to-sit/

Madson, MA, CBCC-KA, CPDT-KA, C. (2020, July 25). *How To Teach Your Dog To Come When Called.* Https://Www.Preventivevet.Com/. https://www.preventivevet.com/dogs/how-to-teach-your-dog-to-come-when-called

Recall Training. (n.d.). Https://Www.Doglistener.Co.Uk. https://www.doglistener.co.uk/behavioural/recall_training.shtml

Simply Behaviour. (n.d.). *Simply Behaviour.* Http://Www.Simplybehaviour.Com/. http://www.simplybehaviour.com/

Yin, D. S. (n.d.). *Teaching Rover To Race To You In Cue.* Cattledog Publishing. https://drsophiayin.com/blog/entry/teaching_rover_to_race_to_you_on_cue/

https://www.thelabradorsite.com/teaching-a-dog-to-heel/

Salonen, M., Sulkama, S., Mikkola, S. et al. *Prevalence, comorbidity, and breed differences in canine anxiety in 13,700 Finnish pet dogs. Sci Rep* 10, 2962 (2020). https://doi.org/10.1038/s41598-020-59837-z

Barbara L. Sherman, Daniel S. Mills, *Canine Anxieties and Phobias: An Update on Separation Anxiety and Noise Aversions, Veterinary Clinics of North America*: Small Animal Practice, Volume 38, Issue 5, 2008, Pages 1081-1106, ISSN 0195-5616, https://doi.org/10.1016/j.cvsm.2008.04.012

Blue Cross For Pets, Retrieved from https://www.bluecross.org.uk/pet-advice/home-alone-separation-anxiety-dogs

Tiira, Katriina & Lohi, Hannes. (2015). *Early Life Experiences and Exercise Associate with Canine Anxieties. PloS one.* 10. e0141907. 10.1371/journal.pone.0141907. Retrieved from https://www.

researchgate.net/publication/283492761_Early_Life_Experiences_and_Exercise_Associate_with_Canine_Anxieties

Dog Psychology 101, https://dogpsychology101.com/

Pet Poison Helpline https://www.petpoisonhelpline.com/pet-owners/emergency/

Made in the USA
Middletown, DE
08 June 2022